Measuring Up:

The Promises and Pitfalls of Performance Indicators in Higher Education

by Gerald Gaither, Brian P. Nedwek, and John E. Neal

ASHE-ERIC Higher Education Report No. 5, 1994

Prepared by

Clearinghouse on Higher Education
The George Washington University

In cooperation with

Association for the Study
of Higher Education

Published by

Graduate School of Education and Human Development
The George Washington University

Jonathan D. Fife, Series Editor

Cite as

Gaither, Gerald, Brian P. Nedwek, and John E. Neal. 1994.
Measuring Up: The Promises and Pitfalls of Performance Indicators in Higher Education. ASHE-ERIC Higher Education
Report No. 5. Washington, D.C.: The George Washington University, Graduate School of Education and Human
Development.

Library of Congress Catalog Card Number 95-79711
ISSN 0884-0040
ISBN 1-878380-61-3

Managing Editor: Bryan Hollister
Manuscript Editor: Barbara Fishel, Editech
Cover design by Michael David Brown, Rockville, Maryland

The ERIC Clearinghouse on Higher Education invites individuals to submit proposals for writing monographs for the
ASHE-ERIC Higher Education Report series. Proposals must
include:
1. A detailed manuscript proposal of not more than five pages.
2. A chapter-by-chapter outline.
3. A 75-word summary to be used by several review committees for the initial screening and rating of each proposal.
4. A vita and a writing sample.

ERIC Clearinghouse on Higher Education
Graduate School of Education and Human Development
The George Washington University
One Dupont Circle, Suite 630
Washington, DC 20036-1183

This publication was prepared partially with funding from
the Office of Educational Research and Improvement, U.S.
Department of Education, under contract no. ED RR-93-0200.
The opinions expressed in this report do not necessarily
reflect the positions or policies of OERI or the Department.

EXECUTIVE SUMMARY

When Adam walked with Eve in the Garden of Eden, he
was overheard to say (presumably by the angel just arrived
with the flaming sword), "You must understand, my dear,
that we are living through a period of transition" (Gray
1951, p. 213).

This volume is also about transitions and issues unfolding
during the implementation of performance indicators. Beginning in the 1980s, the era concerned primarily with growth
in enrollments and access was largely over, while another
waited further definition and recognition in such emerging
issues as public accountability, quality, productivity, and
undergraduate education.

The 1980s was also distinguished by the growth of the
movement toward assessment and accountability. While
higher education in the United States was affected by several
phenomena during this decade, surely none created more
fundamental change than the movement toward assessment.
A 1990 study by the Education Commission of the States, for
example, revealed that 40 states actively promoted assessment
(Ewell, Finney, and Lenth 1990). Along with this movement
was a rising interest in the quality of undergraduate education,
and a litany of studies published in the 1980s lamented the
poor condition of undergraduate education, pointing to
inadequacies that needed to be corrected (see, e.g., Association of American 1985; Bennett 1984; Boyer 1987; Levine
and Boyer 1981; Sykes 1988). By 1986, all 50 states and the
District of Columbia had developed initiatives to improve
undergraduate education (Boyer and McGuinness 1986).

Accompanying this movement was a subtle shift from
growth in funding, principally through formula funding,
toward funding "outcomes," "results," and "performance."
This focus on performance, using funding incentives as motivators, helped encourage policy makers and the academic
community to explore the use of a system of indicators to
raise warning signs about the efficiency and effectiveness of
higher education.

These domestic efforts paralleled developments in higher
education in a number of countries, particularly in Europe
and Australia. Since the late 1970s, the concepts of performance indicators and quality assessment have clearly become
international issues (Dochy, Segers, and Wijnen 1990a, 1990b;
Kells 1993). Indeed, they are becoming an integral part of

an emerging international method on how to manage higher education, with indicators serving as signals or guides for making national or international comparisons in educational quality, effectiveness, and efficiency (National Center for Education 1994a; Sizer, Spee, and Bormans 1992). Further, the main advantage of such performance indicator systems is their usefulness as points of reference for comparing quality or performance against peers over time, or achievement against a desired objective.

The 1990s emerged as part of another era awaiting further definition. First, the development of performance indicators in the 1990s differs from that in the 1980s. Policy makers are generally less inclined toward the voluntary institutional improvement of the 1980s and more focused on a system of mandated public accountability. And by 1994 some 18 states had developed indicator systems, most of them in the first three years of the decade (Ewell 1994a). A heightened tempo in the use of performance indicators, accompanied by a tendency to copy other states' systems, resulted in a common core of state indicators to address common problems. Concomitant with this movement was greater centralization of authority, with the intent of bringing about more public accountability and better management—which will likely underlie much future funding of higher education in the United States.

The air is full of questions. Will the federal government assume greater centralized control of higher education through such areas as accreditation and financial aid and by using a set of national goals and performance standards? Will international education continue to be reformed through the mechanisms of performance indicators and incentive funding? How should such mechanisms be best used to motivate and bring about desired reforms on campus and at state, regional, or national levels? While scholars and legislators debate these questions, the public's investment in and concern about quality and performance in higher education continue unabated, and institutional resistance to fundamental reform remains ingrained. It remains unclear whether performance indicators and incentive funding will result in any widespread, lasting innovations or the concept will pass quickly through higher education in this country, leaving only a modest residue.

Perhaps, however, a hint about any lasting contribution and the future role for performance indicators can be found in Europe, where early pioneering efforts on quality assessment are maturing. Nationally, the role of performance indicators is declining (Green 1994; Jongbloed and Westerheijden 1994), and growing doubts about the ability to "measure the unmeasurable," particularly about the validity of such measures to evaluate and be used to reward quality, have led to retrenchment in such countries as the Netherlands and the United Kingdom. At the same time, national and institutional experiments with such assessment techniques as peer reviews and quality audits are gaining prominence, relegating performance indicators to the role of supporting tools in such efforts (Green 1994; Jongbloed and Westerheijden 1994).

This emerging approach offers the collective faculty a more palatable, more dynamic vision of academic quality, ostensibly more worthy of their commitment and pursuit than any externally imposed system of performance indicators (Burke 1994). Faculty resolutely insist they know academic quality when they see it and should retain the primary responsibility for assessing and rewarding it. But such autonomy is always purchased by providing measures of accountability for results and resources to the public and to policy makers. It remains to be seen whether faculty will assume the collective mantle of responsibility and professional obligation to develop processes that develop a sense of common purpose and shared accountability with the various publics. If this pattern gains prominence, performance indicators will likely be relegated to a minor role as a supporting tool; if the academy does not respond, the public appetite for results will expand and crystallize around the use of external performance indicators to measure desired results. And the jury is still out on the results desired.

CONTENTS

The increasing demand for quantifiable evidence that higher education is worth the cost and the time involved is a result of three major economic and social changes of the last three decades. First, a higher education has become considerably more import in securing and keeping a good-paying job than it was 30 years ago. For society as a whole, the quality of higher education institutions is crucial to the nation's ability to compete economically with the other countries of the world. Second, consumers have become more sophisticated. The more college graduates and the more students with parents who are college graduates, the less willing are consumers to accept the effectiveness of their education on faith, especially when they believe their personal expectations for an education are not being met. Students are no longer willing to accept that the faculty's professional expertise should allow them to make decisions that affect their lives without some evidence of the validity and reliability of those decisions. Third, the cost of higher education is greater than it was 30 years ago. Higher education is taking an increasingly large portion of disposable or discretionary income of both individuals and public funding agencies. As decisions about spending become harder and more painful to make, people naturally want information to help them decide where they should put their money. The consequence is greater demand for quantitative data about how well higher education is performing. But what should be measured, and how will this measurement be used?

Three types of performance indicators can be used to judge the quality of any process. The type most often used is the measurement of results—for higher education, for example, the percentage of students graduating, the number of degrees awarded, the percentage of students going on to graduate schools, or the number of publications by faculty. These measures do not indicate a sense of quality, however, only quantity. Increasingly, the expectation is now to measure the quality or degree of the outcome—"measuring the value added"— exemplified by how many students went to the best graduate schools, their average starting salary compared to comparable schools, or the number of faculty publications cited in the publications of other scholars.

The second measure of performance is the quality of inputs: SAT or ACT scores of entering students, their rank in class or recognition as a merit scholar, the rank of faculty members' graduate degree programs, whether faculty brought with them research grants, or the number of refereed publications. The theory behind indicators of this type is that if the quality of input is high, then results will be high.

The third set of measurements that has become increasingly important as performance indicators is measurement of or at critical process points. This new emphasis is a result of concern with the other two types of measurement. When only outcomes or results are measured, then it is too late to do anything but accept or reject the situation. For many, the realization that 50 percent of starting students never achieve their education goals is no longer acceptable. Research has shown that if a process is flawed, highly satisfactory results will not be ensured even if the process starts with quality students and faculty. Consequently, the process of education is receiving increasing scrutiny through indicators such as how often students use the library each week, participate in study groups, hold positions of leadership, write papers, or consult with their academic adviser. For faculty, process indicators could be the number of hours they use to prepare for class, their use of new technology in teaching, or how they validate their assessment of students.

The demand for and use of performance indicators are the foci of *Measuring Up: The Promises and Pitfalls of Performance Indicators in Higher Education.* Gerald Gaither, director of institutional research at the Prairie View campus of the Texas A&M University system, Brian P. Nedwek, associate provost and professor of public policy studies at Saint Louis University, and John E. Neal, associate vice president at Webster University in Saint Louis, have synthesized the most important literature concerning the use of various performance indicators and their possible shortcomings. They look at the experiences of higher education in the United States and then review the development and use of performance indicators in Great Britain, Canada, Australia, the Netherlands, Finland, Sweden, and Denmark. The authors' conclusions provide a direction that could help higher education institutions in this country develop more effective ways to measure the quality of their efforts.

The trend is clear and irreversible: Higher education institutions must start developing better ways to judge more adequately how well they are doing. Higher education has been reluctant to develop performance indicators because, it is believed, the mission of higher education is too diverse to measure and short-term measurement might not be adequate to measure long-term success. If the members of the academy—faculty, academic leaders, students—do not participate in the process of developing and improving the use of performance indicators, however, external organizations will force some form of indicators on them. This report provides a broad perspective that will be useful in establishing an understanding of the issues surrounding the use of performance indicators.

Jonathan D. Fife
Series Editor, Professor of Higher Education Administration, and Director, ERIC Clearinghouse on Higher Education

ACKNOWLEDGMENTS

This publication was prepared partially with a Faculty Mini-Grant from the Prairie View A&M University Research Enhancement Program, which was funded by the Texas Higher Education Coordinating Board. Indirectly, a project supported by the Fund for the Improvement of Postsecondary Education (grant no. P116A41490) also contributed to the research in this monograph.

This book is dedicated to our spouses.

THE POLICY CONNECTION: Ideas and Actions

An invasion of armies can be resisted, but not an idea
whose time has come.
                    —Victor Hugo, *Histoire d'un Crime*

Some Background Issues

State-level quality incentives and performance indicators are
receiving increased attention nationwide among higher education policy makers and planners. Consider:

- Under the rubric of "the accountability imperative," several states have now passed laws that require institutions
  to demonstrate effectiveness, efficiency, sound fiscal stewardship, and proven performance (Ewell 1990, 1994a;
  Lively 1992).
- A 1990 study by the Education Commission of the States
  reveals that 40 states actively promoted assessment (Ewell,
  Finney, and Lenth 1990).
- A later report by the American Council on Education notes
  that 97 percent of all institutions claim to engage in assessment (Marchese 1994, p. 4).
- As of 1992, 19 states required public colleges and universities to set up programs to assess what students learn
  in college (*Chronicle* 1992).
- Eleven of the 15 states in the Southern Regional Education
  Board (SREB) have passed legislation in the past decade
  related to assessment, quality, and/or performance reporting (Lively 1992).

The issues of quality and performance indicators have cap-
tured the attention of those in higher education, revealing
a certain tension among campuses, states, and the public.
Prompting much interest in these topics are, among other
things, reduced public confidence in education, shrinking
state budgets, taxpayers' complaints about rising costs and
taxes, and concern at both the state and national levels about
the loss of economic competitiveness, partially as a result of
the perceived erosion in educational quality. (Although public
confidence in primarily all large organizations in the United
States has eroded in an *absolute* sense since the beginning
of the 1980s, organizations like organized labor, organized

religion, and congress have generally suffered a much greater *relative* erosion of public confidence than has education.)*

While a large gap exists on many campuses between these legal mandates and the reality of assessment, the move toward assessment has helped create a notion of excellence based on goal-oriented performance, sometimes rewarded with funding. Tennessee's classic goal-oriented performance funding model, which was legislated in 1984, is still a prototype for other states. Indeed, the SREB helps to prepare model legislation to allow states to develop "good practices" with respect to accountability and educational quality, particularly at the undergraduate level. As early as 1987, the state of Texas moved toward consideration of incentive funding, and later performance funding, as part of this "good practices" effort (Ashworth 1994; Bateman and Elliott 1994; Gaither 1993). Arkansas is developing a system of productivity goals, Missouri is developing performance funding under the aegis of "funding for results," and South Carolina and Virginia use "report cards" on effectiveness, ostensibly logical first steps along the road to incentive or performance funding. Outside the SREB, Colorado in 1993 adopted a form of incentive funding to reward institutions for exemplary performance that matches state goals (Lively 1994). As of 1994, some 18 states had a system of state-based higher education performance indicators in place, most of which had been developed within the previous three years (Ewell 1994a, p. 147), and it seems likely that this approach will be used increasingly across the country (Ashworth 1994, p. 11).

These related concepts of assessment, performance indicators, and performance funding have the same intended goal: to require institutions of higher education to demonstrate accountability and achievement of their missions and goals. They are often also designed, however, to influence universities' and colleges' priorities and their achievement of their mission as teachers of undergraduates. The external attention focused on these concepts has fueled an internal campus drive for better academic performance, particularly in the delivery of undergraduate teaching (Bogue and Saunders 1992; Forum 1990). In response to a litany of studies pub-

---

*Tom Smith, director, General Social Survey, National Opinion Research Center, University of Chicago. Correspondence May 28, 1993, and telephone conversation March 23, 1994.

lished in the 1980s lamenting the poor condition of undergraduate education and pointing to inadequacies needing correction (see, e.g., Association of American 1985; Bennett 1984; Boyer 1987; Levine and Boyer 1981; Sykes 1988), a report on undergraduate education by the Education Commission of the States (1990) calls for each institution to develop "its own indicators of effectiveness" that would reflect the "institution's distinctive undergraduate mission" and provides a list of suggested indicators to afford "some comparability across institutions of similar missions" (see also Boyer et al. 1986 and Evangelauf 1986).

Public concern, particularly about the quality of instruction, reached governors and legislators, and by 1986 all 50 states and the District of Columbia had developed initiatives to improve undergraduate education (Boyer and McGuinness 1986). The public's interest in linking funding with specific results also helped prompt legislators to act. "Much of the impetus behind [such] assessment is the desire by state leaders to hold colleges and universities accountable for achieving their educational purposes and for expending their funds" (Gaff 1991, p. 58). Earlier management systems and their built-in funding motivators rewarded growth and spending over effectiveness and efficiency, for when government agencies, including public higher education, receive their appropriations on input-type funding formulas, "they have little reason to strive for better performance" (Osborne and Gaebler 1993, p. 140). The resulting shift, almost imperceptible in some quarters, was toward "results-oriented government"— that is, funding outcomes, not inputs—and words like "performance" and "results" began to enter the lexicon of government (p. 349) (see, e.g., Barrett and Greene 1992; McKenna 1991, 1993; Sharp 1993).

This focus on performance and incentives helped encourage policy makers and the academic community to explore the use of indicators to measure performance—or at least to raise warning signs about the efficiency and effectiveness of education in serving the needs of its various constituencies. In particular, increasing emphasis has been placed over the past decade on the formal assessment of institutional performance and the use of funding, usually in limited amounts, as an incentive and reward for high performance and achievement of state goals (Brinkman 1982; Green 1984; Howell 1987; Hyatt and Santiago 1984; Hyde 1983; McMahon 1986).

The public's interest in linking funding with specific results also helped prompt legislators to act.

Institutional assessment without a link to funding had only limited success and was not as far-reaching as policy makers desired or anticipated. In the final analysis, incentive funding programs in the 1980s were accepted in only modest doses as components of strategic change and quality reform (Holland and Berdahl 1990). Growing fiscal problems in several states in the late 1980s added to the demise of such programs; in New Jersey, for example, revenue shortfalls had eroded incentive funding by 1990 (Hollander 1991).

These domestic efforts parallel general developments in higher education in a number of countries, particularly in Europe (Great Britain and the Netherlands) and Australia (Hüfner and Rau 1987; Kells 1992b, 1993; Sizer, Spee, and Bormans 1992), and since the late 1970s, the concepts of performance indicators and quality assessment have clearly become international issues (Dochy, Segers, and Wijnen 1990a; Kells 1990, 1992b, 1993). They are becoming an integral part of an emerging international method on how to better manage and assess higher education, and they serve as signals or guides for making national or international comparisons in educational quality, effectiveness, and efficiency (Burke 1993a, p. 28; National Center for Education 1994a; Sizer, Spee, and Bormans 1992). In Europe and Australia, the use of indicators generally remains at the national level, while in the United States, performance indicators have remained largely the province of the states. That pattern could change in the 1990s, however, if federal edicts are deemed necessary to supplement lagging state and institutional efforts to provide a concept of quality based on performance and results (Edgerton 1991).

The concepts of assessment produced in Australia, the Netherlands, and the United Kingdom were primarily the product of government ideology in the context of quality assessment; such indicators have tended to reflect the country's and the period's ideologies, and they were developed in response to educational issues of the day (Darling-Hammond 1992). Such government efforts to use indicators as policy levers or methods of control are ill-advised, and to be effective, they must first reflect educational activities and institutional processes if they are to serve a larger, more constructive policy role (Darling-Hammond 1992). Others emphasized the use of such indicators in measuring "goal congruence" between the institutions and government, suggesting that indicators could be best used as "indications of perfor-mance" and not precise statistical measures (Sizer, Spee, and Bormans 1992). The emphasis in this volume is on the results of such indicators as "signals," not absolute statistical meas-urements. Thus, the term "performance indicators" seems preferable to "performance measures," because the latter invests the concept with an impossible precision. State and institutional assessment goals in the United States might not be as far apart as often assumed (Richardson 1994a); thus, the initial tensions brought about by the introduction of qual-ity indicators could be resolved with time.

The specific reasons for adoption of these concepts varied from country to country and from state to state. In Australia, for example, performance indicators were developed to encourage education to better respond to government prior-ities (Dochy, Segers, and Wijnen 1990a; Kells 1992b). The government embraced the concept with such enthusiasm that the Australian Vice Chancellors Committee and the Association of College Directors and Principals issued a word of caution:

> Something resembling a . . . cult seems to have grown up around the notion of performance indicators, so that all manner of powers and virtues are ascribed to them and expectations are aroused that by collecting and using them great benefits will miraculously result. This erroneous atti-tude arises when performance indicators are considered in isolation and out of the context in which they should properly be used (Teather 1990a, p. 103).

The Netherlands embraced performance indicators and quality assessment primarily as a result of the economic crisis in that country during the early 1980s. In response to asser-tions that education and research, which consume approx-imately 20 percent of the government's annual budget, are highly inefficient, higher education had to put its economic house in order to relieve the pressure on the country's expen-ditures. A new managerial system using performance indi-cators was regarded as a way to bring needed fiscal respon-siveness and discipline to Dutch higher education. As part of the desired response, for example, institutions began pro-ducing "fact books" containing such information as graduation rates, student/faculty ratios, and personnel profiles (Maassen and van Vught 1988; Spee and Bormans 1992). To reward this responsiveness, a new quality control system, which linked increased autonomy with greater quality control, went into legal effect in August 1993 (Sander 1993).

The concept of indicators reached fruition in the United Kingdom by the late 1980s. The use of performance indicators was highly correlated with the rise of Margaret Thatcher as prime minister and her insistence on government agencies' being more responsive to the free market. Thatcher (and others, including Ronald Reagan in the United States) indicated that the education system should be more self-reliant and more dependent on market forces, rather than merely looking for ever greater government support without accountability (Goedegebuure, Maassen, and Westerheijden 1990a; Temple and Whitechurch 1994). While the United Kingdom demanded more responsiveness to market priorities and Australia demanded more response to government priorities, both countries focused almost concurrently on the use of performance indicators as a point from which to make their academic and managerial assessments of educational performance.

In the United States, the Wisconsin and State University of New York (SUNY) systems were rewarded during the late 1980s and early 1990s with greater autonomy by their respective state legislatures for responding to legislative concerns before policy makers flexed their legal muscle (Ruppert 1994e). In 1988, for example, then-Provost Joseph Burke of SUNY launched an initiative focused on assessment that had as its major goals the improvement of teaching, the evaluation of the university's effectiveness, and the measurement of learning outcomes. While not mandated by the state, the effort has provided convincing evidence to governors, legislators, and the general public that SUNY is producing desired results without legislation.

Although the reasons for their use vary from country to country, the concepts of quality assessment and quality indicators and their use as an integral part of planning, allocation, and assessment are quite similar.

A key factor in the international emergence of performance indicators is their side effect on the rapid growth and progress of international technology. User-friendly, accessible, prolific, and comprehensive data systems were key factors in the emergence of performance indicators (Lucier 1992). What was available was collected and measured. What was measured—

or measurable—was given value, and what was given value was reviewed for accountability and funding. Just as there is or should be a link between planning and budgeting, the proliferation of sophisticated information technology, beginning in the 1980s, was linked—or at least highly correlated—to the rise and use of performance indicators. While the concept of indicators arrived slightly earlier in Europe than in the United States and has become more widely entrenched there, the lack of information technology at the same level of sophistication as in the United States has made Europe and other countries lag somewhat behind some of the more sophisticated efforts in the United States.

This strong tilt toward accountability and assessment in various countries shared some common themes of development and implementation with many states in the United States during the middle to late 1980s. One characteristic of the move toward assessment in the United States was "the incredible speed of its evolution" (Ewell 1993a, p. 12), and by 1989, 15 states had some form of legislation on measures of student outcomes, with 13 having pending legislation (Sims 1992, p. 56). Another pattern in the United States that emulated the European process was the tendency to use "legislation by fax" (Ewell 1993a, p. 12). Imitation became the sincerest form of flattery in much of the legislation mandating assessment. For example, New Mexico's "report card bill" was parroted in South Carolina's Act 225, and Kentucky's SB109 subsequently emulated South Carolina's act—suggesting a pattern of communication and commonality in legislation and data items collected by the various states, much the same way that it occurred in Europe between countries.

As a result, both mistakes and some factors worth emulating were transplanted across states. For example, one commonly used or considered state performance measure or indicator (e.g., in Texas, South Carolina, Wisconsin, and Tennessee) emphasizes senior or experienced faculty's teaching lower-division courses, with the implicit implication that senior faculty are "better" teachers. Little evidence based on research suggests this assumption is correct, however (Feldman 1983).

Other states or systems (e.g., Colorado, New York, Kentucky, and Florida) use indicator systems that assume lower student/faculty ratios or smaller class sizes are associated with a greater cognitive gain in learning (see, e.g., Ewell 1994a, p. 156). Despite such ostensibly common conceptions by the

public and policy makers alike, the literature fails to link small class size or lower student/faculty ratios with increased learning gains in the classroom (Dubin and Taveggia 1968; McKeachie 1980; Tomlinson 1988; Williams et al. 1985). True, overwhelming research results indicate students *believe* they learn more and are more satisfied with smaller classes or a lower student/faculty ratio, but little research evidence validates these impressions (Ewell 1993b, pp. 16–17). Would indicator systems with incentives that enhance learning productivity through more self-paced instruction or greater use of technology be more effective in producing the desired results?

Finally, another common flaw in indicator systems is their tendency to reward (or punish) a single institution for students' summative performance. Holding degree-granting institutions totally responsible for the competency of their graduates is a logical, but mind-boggling, research problem for performance indicators. Assessments of the source and quality of student learning outcomes in general or of remedial education courses, for example, are particularly difficult to determine in comprehensive colleges, doctorate-granting institutions, or research universities. Many, if not most, students in such institutions do not take the majority of their general education courses at the institution from which they receive their degree (Smith 1993). Further, the courses taken by students at a community college do not produce the same results as those taken at a baccalaureate-granting institution (Ratcliff 1992, p. 65). Transfer students are generally not separated from native students when summative competencies are evaluated. In short, an assumption of a common intellectual experience by graduates of a particular institution is interwoven into many indicator systems, and the validity seems dubious of a statewide indicator system with incentives and rewards tied to the learning gains by students of a single institution and not a collection of experiences.

And herewith lies a problem with some performance indicators: They often lack validity and reliability. The tendency to imitate other programs sometimes creates a tendency to adopt unproven measures or indicators not based on research findings. On the positive side, however, such imitation suggests common perceptions of problems that extend beyond state borders as well as policy makers' willingness to act promptly on solutions.

The Quality Revolution

The 1980s witnessed the emergence of a spirited public debate about quality, not only in higher education, but also in the corporate sector. The media were filled with criticisms of current practice, with calls for improvement, and with particular concerns about the U.S. market's vulnerability to Japanese products (see, e.g., Kennedy 1993; Porter 1990; Thurow 1993). The debate proved frustrating, not only because the voices became strident, but also because the responding messages were often contradictory. At the same time, for example, that the Ford Motor Company proudly proclaimed "Quality Is Job One," the company was recalling its products as a result of faulty manufacturing and assembly. Fingers were pointed not only at industry but also at education—and rightly so. Students' math and verbal and written expression skills were weak across the nation, and standardized test scores had declined nearly 80 points in the previous three decades as spending increased significantly (Barton 1994; Bennett 1993; Murray and Herrnstein 1992). The percentage of education budgets devoted to remedial and developmental education was also increasing, and the resulting quality of students, to the public eye, did not seem to be improving. Indeed, if many of those students had been automobiles, they likely would have been recalled by the high schools or colleges from which they graduated. Remedial or developmental education programs in the three R's to bring high school graduates up to college-entry skills became common on college campuses by the end of the 1980s (Clowes 1992, p. 460). Public opinion clearly reflected a highly critical attitude toward educational malpractice. It was "the first time since the late 1950s that the American people [were] so aroused about the quality of education" (Gaff 1991, p. 5). In view of such widespread remediation, it is not surprising that college-educated Americans are not very literate. A summary of 2,600 studies on higher education outcomes by the Educational Testing Service Policy Information Center found that:

- About half of college graduates cannot understand a bus schedule.
- Only 13 percent of college graduates can perform multiple-step math problems.
- Only 11 percent of four-year graduates and 4 percent of

two-year graduates can properly summarize a passage on how lawyers challenge prospective jurors (Barton 1994).

The budget does reflect public values and national priorities for higher education (Albright 1985, p. 16; Bogue 1993; Folger 1984b, p. 1; see also Darling-Hammond 1992). During the 1960s and 1970s, for example, national goals for higher education addressed social injustices and expanded access. Efforts to increase minority enrollments and financial aid programs, with low tuition rates to support increased enrollments, were the order of the day. Budget mechanisms, primarily funding formulas, were prevalent as a means of promoting growth in higher education and equity in the allocation of resources (McKeown 1989; Moss and Gaither 1976; Noe 1986). Input variables, such as enrollments, were emphasized. And accreditation reviews favored such input variables as volumes in the library and number of faculty with terminal degrees.

But with the 1980s and the public's perceived erosion of quality in education, the goals for higher education shifted in almost epidemic proportions to a focus on quality—by the academy and the public alike. From January 1983 to December 1990, for example, ERIC lists 13,541 publications explicitly referring to "quality" in education (Noble, Cryns, and Laury 1992, p. 310). In 1986, a task force of the National Governors Association concluded that, among other things, governors, state legislatures, and coordinating boards should adjust input-oriented funding formulas to provide incentives for improving the quality of undergraduate education, based on the results of a comprehensive assessment program (Sims 1992, p. 52).

National goals for higher education in the 1980s—indeed, to the present—remain much the same as they were in the 1960s and 1970s, with an emphasis on equity, access, and student financial need (Mingle 1989, p. 8). But even at the federal level, at least by the late 1990s, performance evaluation in the form of peer reviews and assessments by external agencies can be expected to intensify. This trend at the federal level toward greater accountability for federal funds will probably result in universities' being *required* to examine their priorities and perhaps restrict their organizations to achieve greater efficiency without compromising effectiveness.

Reforming the process of accreditation appears to be a current focus as the federal government expands its involvement in performance assessment. In December 1993, the Council on Postsecondary Accreditation (COPA), the major membership organization for accrediting agencies, was disbanded. Part H of the Program Integrity Triad of the Reauthorized Higher Education Act of 1965 portends growing federal intrusion in accreditation, as institutions participating in the Student Financial Aid Program of Title IV are subject to governmental reviews of curriculum, student personnel policies, and quality assurances, once the purview of accrediting agencies and institutions. In sum, the federal government appears on the verge of no longer leaving evidence of quality and licensure to state and accrediting agencies (Sims 1992), suggesting a growing federalization of higher education—a common phenomenon in Europe, but a radical shift in U.S. educational policy. Particularly for private and independent institutions, this shift represents a dangerous intrusion into campus operations and could precipitate the homogenization of higher education in the United States. Indeed, the movement toward state assessment was partly a response to national concerns about quality, but it might be too little too late. Higher education ostensibly must prepare for a three-tier system of review that includes national baseline standards, state performance standards, and accreditation standards for recognition of overall excellence. And reports of such findings are likely to become public, communicating institutional strengths and weaknesses to a broad segment of the public—and acting as an incentive for change or as a rallying point to crystallize institutional opposition to external review.

Another national effort, although still largely symbolic, is expansion of the Malcolm Baldrige National Quality Award, handed out annually by the U.S. Department of Commerce, to include schools, colleges, and hospitals. Plans are to have a pilot contest in 1995, with no winners announced, and a full contest in 1996 (Fuchsberg 1993a). Because measures of quality in education and health care are not as well defined as they are in business, this award and the criteria to be established are sure to be controversial. Questions are also being raised as to whether such a "quality contest" creates the right incentives for change, and concerns are being voiced that the criteria, once established, could become a set of national performance standards for *all* educational institutions. A national indicator system could be in our future as a result of this climate for a fuller accounting of how well institutions of higher education are preparing their students and using their resources (Edgerton 1991).

From the perspective of the states, however, the educational agenda in the 1980s had already shifted to such issues as assessment, more selective admissions and stratification among institutions, the core curriculum, better undergraduate education, merit scholarships, incentive funding—and a greater emphasis on quality. "The elixir of the 1980s was quality" (Mingle 1989, p. 8).

In the 1960s, funding formulas were the budget vehicle the states used to promote growth and access, while performance or incentive funding, which emerged in the 1980s, was generally designed to *supplement* the still widely existing formula allocation system and to promote greater effectiveness. Further, the formula system was designed primarily around enrollment-driven *input* or activity measures, while performance and incentive funding generally encouraged institutions to measure *outcomes,* a much more slippery and abstract activity that has proved elusive, difficult to define, multifaceted, and much more expensive and uncertain for planners to measure. In Florida, for example, higher education officials estimated that two systemwide reports required by a 1991 "accountability" law would cost $1.3 million to develop through new software and student evaluation forms. Florida officials say they cannot afford such additional expenditures when budgets for course offerings and libraries are being cut. In South Carolina, institutional research directors estimated it would cost $20,000 for each institution to compile a "report card" that measures the performance of higher education (Blumenstyk 1993).

Thus, these outcomes and prescriptions based on quality often come at a price: external agencies' greater intrusion in academic issues and institutions' absorption of new costs. Faculty and administrators alike should remember that this external concern for accountability in state capitals and in Washington has emerged, in part, because of the academy's partial default on its professional obligations to produce the desired results and inform the public and students.

The Productivity Challenge

As quality became a national concern in the 1980s, the word took on political implications among policy makers. But along with the public's and state leaders' rising concern about quality came a concomitant concern about cost and productivity in higher education (Hollins 1992). These same external policy groups often included the concept of "productivity" under the umbrella of quality (Mingle 1989). This connection and the vocabulary itself are largely anathema to many faculty, however, who view suspiciously the unwelcome overlap between the values of higher education and business—a distinction between the service and the profit sectors.

The twin issues of quality and productivity have been interrelated since the 1980s, and the concern appears to be strengthening among state leaders who seek concrete results and indicators of "service to the state." To many state leaders, a quality institution is a productive institution, providing measurable returns for the state's economic aid in the form of research dollars, training, and service. A study of the SUNY system (Slaughter 1985) confirms that faculty's expected role has shifted since 1970 from primarily serving students to serving the state's economy. Faculty in the study were expected to be more productive, for example, by linking their research to industrial revitalization, to train students for "high-tech, high-cost, high-return" jobs. In the main, faculty are being asked to be more "productive" to help states overcome their fiscal problems by revitalizing their industrial bases. Performance indicators to measure an institution's contribution to a state's economic goals are becoming more common (see, e.g., Ashworth 1994, p. 14; Borden and Banta 1994; Ewell 1994a, p. 157).

A study confirms that SUNY faculty's expected role has shifted from primarily serving students to serving the state's economy.

But the broader discussions about what represents a productive institution are hazy and fragmented (Hodgkinson 1981). Current discussions tend to take at least two distinct perspectives. One group tends to focus more on institutional *efficiency* and a more *quantitative* approach in which productivity means working harder and faster and producing more measurable units of what is produced. An increase in faculty credit hours or research dollars over the previous year, for example, would be an acceptable increase in productivity that would include measures or performance indicators to evaluate the desired results. The public and other constituencies beyond the campus prefer this viewpoint.

A second perspective on productivity is more concerned with *effectiveness* and continuous *improvement* in quality, for while "efficiency does not include effectiveness, . . . effectiveness does include efficiency" (Burke 1993b, p. 4). Within the world of higher education, this definition is the more palatable one. Measures like the amount of published, refereed research produced, enhanced prestige among peers, improved college ratings and rankings, greater amounts of·resources, and an increase in the number of citation indices, for example, represent a "productive" institution (Bogue and Saunders 1992, p. 65; Cave, Hanney, and Kogan 1991, pp. 128–35; Eash 1983; Jalongo 1985). Clearly, these two viewpoints about productivity overlap, but one theme or the other seems more dominant with certain constituencies.

For example, concurrent with the concern about the quality of undergraduate education is a widespread belief that faculty workloads are declining and that the time spent by full-time faculty in the classroom is declining (Jacobson 1992; Jordan and Layzell 1992; Russell 1992). A study of faculty workload in 1993 conducted by the Ohio Board of Regents found that teaching loads had dropped 10 percent in the previous decade in state institutions. The result was legislation to increase the amount of time faculty devoted to undergraduate education (Magner 1994). In Texas, the Coordinating Board for Higher Education developed and the legislature adopted as one of its performance indicators a semester-by-semester report to the Legislative Budget Board about the percentage of time full-time faculty spend with lower-division courses.

Paradoxically, as faculty workloads ostensibly declined, the workload of the "average" American was increasing. Today the average worker works one extra month per year compared to 20 years ago (Schoor 1991). And the increased workload has been accompanied by an increase in the number of people working—a necessity to maintain comparable standards of living. From 1972 to 1992, the number of two-earner households rose 41 percent, the number of single-parent wage earners 156 percent (Schoor 1991). This increased workload in the private sector could help explain the public's and policy makers' growing scrutiny and criticism of the neglect of teaching in favor of research.

The charge that some faculty are unproductive, inefficient, and incompetent becomes more tenable when some data are examined. A national study of workload conducted by the Carnegie Foundation for the Advancement of Teaching concludes that "the average faculty member devotes about 20 hours a week *to* the classroom" but spends only "an average of 9.8 to 10.5 hours a week *in* the classroom." Further, 45 percent of the nation's faculty "had no professional writings accepted or published during a given two-year period" (Maeroff 1993). Although such statistics might be sufficient to label faculty "the new leisure class" (Maeroff 1993), not many inside the academy would agree (Magner 1994, p. A18); nevertheless, as of April 1992 "at least a dozen states" were seeking performance data on faculty work weeks and contact hours (Jacobson 1992).

If individuals respond to financial incentives, then the reasons are clear for undergraduate instruction's suffering. A study of over 4,000 tenure-track faculty at a wide range of institutions reached the following conclusions:

- The more time you spend on teaching, the less compensation.
- The more hours in class per week, the lower the pay.
- The greater the time spent on research, the higher the compensation.
- Faculty who teach only graduate students get paid most.
- The greater the number of refereed publications, the greater the income (Jacobson 1992).

The pervasiveness of the incentive system can be aptly illustrated by a review of the criteria for the SUNY Distinguished Teaching Professorships, which are intended to reward the system's best teachers. The criteria require—and the system-wide committee rigorously enforces—"a substantial record in research and publication" (Burke 1993b, p. 7). In contrast, the Distinguished Professorship, which requires a substantial national record in publications and research, requires no evidence of good teaching skills (p. 7). Clearly, most faculty who do not stress the primary role of research over teaching will not rise to the top of their profession or receive recognition. But "what is truly amazing is that there are so many faculty in research universities who care about teaching despite the virtual absence of rewards for doing so" (Edgerton 1993a, p. 16).

A proposed faculty incentive and reward system would have tenured faculty guaranteed a threshold salary and earning the rest of their salaries each year as rewards for achieving agreed-upon goals (Heydinger and Simsek 1992). Such a system is intended to counter the unintended but obvious ways that current incentives produce prevailing practices.

Analyses of performance and productivity in several studies conclude that much of the reason productivity has declined stems from faculty members' shift toward research and professional activity and away from undergraduate teaching, as prestige in the academic culture comes from research rather than teaching. Although in one study "educational quality" was improved initially as a result of the instructor's research, it subsequently declined, and the final results were an increase in the cost per student, less quality time for undergraduates, and a proliferation of support services. And the relationship drove up costs in academic departments (see, e.g., Hollins 1992; Massy and Meyerson 1994; Massy and Zemsky 1990). Spurred on by such evidence, public policy makers are seeking more public accountability, particularly in relation to undergraduate education.

One of the more innovative campus or system responses to the challenge of productivity comes from SUNY. Despite the need to increase productivity, advances cannot be made by "reducing or cheapening the inputs" (e.g., cutting faculty or staff) or increasing the output (Johnstone 1993a, 1993b). Any "significant and sustainable" increases in productivity must come through the learner's productivity; that is, students' "demonstrated mastery of a defined body of knowledge or skills," for example, by using a set of prescribed measures or indicators for individually paced learning (p. 2). The key ingredients for such a system are (1) a set of clear, comprehensive, and measurable learning objectives; (2) assessment instruments; and (3) moving the student on to a new set of objectives after mastery and measurement of the initial assignment (Johnstone 1993a, 1993b).

Accompanying this concept is SUNY's development of a systemwide set of performance indicators (see table 1). A common set of macro indicators has been developed for institutions in the system, and individual campuses are developing micro indicators that reflect their institutional missions (Richardson 1994f). Along with this system is an accelerated degree program that went into effect at seven of the 64 SUNY campuses during summer 1994. A number of other institutions have followed suit with offerings of three-year degrees that respond more to economics, such as making college more affordable for students, than to any demand for productive learning (Stecklow 1994). This situation is more an anomaly than a common pattern, however, as delay of graduation until

TABLE 1

SOME PERFORMANCE INDICATORS FROM THE
SUNY PERFORMANCE REPORTS

	Indicator	Comparison	Data Source
• Funding context	1. Revenue by source	1. Trend states	1. IPEDS; institutional research
	2. Tuition rate trends	2. Regional/national	2. NASULGC/AASCU surveys
	3. Educational and general expenditures per student	3. Previous years: national, peers, state	3. IPEDS finance survey; institutional research
	4. Benchmark	4. System/SUNY sectors	4. Finance and business; institutional research
• Access to undergraduate education			
—Admissions	Applicants, acceptances	Trends in enrolled/ accepted and race/ ethnicity	Institutional research
—Enrollment	Total, race/ethnicity, level/ age	Previous years, state sectors, high school/graduation trends	Institutional research
• Undergraduate quality (students and institutions)	Assessment plans and pass rates	Previous years	Institutional research
	Basic skills	Periodic reports	Institutional research
	Class size	Trends	

Note: A more extensive list of SUNY's goals and related indicators can be found in Burke 1993a, pp. 31–37.

after five or six years of attendance is not unusual because of students' inability to take the needed courses or the necessity to work to offset rising costs (Dodge 1991).

Such debates about quality and productivity have become common in the majority of states. And this dichotomous perspective about productivity has framed a fundamental debate between policy makers and academicians over public accountability for higher education and the use of performance indicators.

Summary
The 1980s witnessed several attempts to breathe life into the idea of greater accountability for higher education, with the main stimulus for such reforms externally imposed and politically based. This drama unfolded through a number of themes and issues—input versus output, excellence versus

quality, cost versus productivity—all of them accompanied by a concern for the quality of undergraduate instruction.

For example, the earlier concept of excellence centered primarily around the accumulation of resources and an institution's reputation (Burke 1994). Excellence in a college or university depended largely on such input variables as number of faculty publications and grants, students' SAT scores, and the comprehensiveness of their degree programs. One problem with such a structured, narrow definition of an institution, however, is that it is primarily static in nature. It tends to review the condition of a college or university at disparate points in time and adds little to monitoring what an institution produces in terms of outputs and outcomes—that is, results—using such resources. The subsequent emerging notion of quality focused on a more dynamic, more expansive notion of goal-oriented institutional excellence based on performance and continuous improvement, on desired results rather than resources, or on "mission fulfillment" (Bogue and Saunders 1992, p. 279).

Performance indicators emerged partly in response to pressures for colleges and universities to demonstrate desired results for resources provided. This subtle shift from excellence to a new notion of quality, which also incorporated assessment, helped meet the public's and policy makers' demands for more accountability. Yet the transformational aspects of this new notion of quality have failed to inspire or motivate faculty to unite behind a common purpose to ensure achievement of an institution's full potential (Burke 1994).

The speed of these changes and their international parallels are striking, and keeping these interrelated themes separate is probably an impossible task. Overriding all of these concepts is the central idea of greater accountability and achievement of mission and goals, accompanied by disparate methods of incentives and rewards—but with a concentration on evaluation and assessment using indicators to seek and measure performance.

Shifts in sentiment are obvious, however, emphasizing institutional effectiveness and student outcomes (Bogue and Saunders 1992, p. 160), with "the overwhelming public posture for state assessment . . . 'improvement,' not 'accountability'" (Ewell 1990, p. 3). Indeed, the "emerging policy consensus" among state leaders was to act but still retain a willingness "to allow institutions full discretion in such matters" (p. 3).

State policy issues for the 1990s include:

- The assessment of educational performance and outcomes;
- The development of new measures of accountability;
- The improvement of productivity for both management and educators;
- The refocus and revision of campus missions (Bogue 1993, p. 3).

Accompanying these themes is a movement toward greater centralization of authority (some would say interference) by the states and in particular the federal government, and a tendency toward less institutional discretion. Greater public accountability will become increasingly important for the rest of the decade.

Information technology and government's greater involvement and control over education have enhanced the need for and allowed the creation of a refined system of performance indicators (Cave, Hanney, and Kogan 1991, p. 35). The remainder of this book maps the emerging contours of this reform movement and details some of the major domestic and international accomplishments to date as well as emerging trends.

PERFORMANCE INDICATORS IN THE UNITED STATES

A number of new players in the United States have fashioned broader, more diverse clusters of performance indicator systems. In addition to the SUNY and the University of Wisconsin systems' projects, previously mentioned, other broader-based models have appeared from which national, state, system, or institutional efforts might be constructed. These efforts constitute a useful reference point for reviewing indicator systems, present or proposed. Although many indicator systems have some potential flaws, particularly with reference to the use of indicators that lack validity and reliability, individual campuses can still profit from these efforts. Indeed, "a set of national benchmarks about key experiences and conditions in general education . . . might be of considerable value in determining the degree to which colleges and universities are able to act consistently with . . . national goals" (Ewell 1993b, p. 5). While "all organizations make mistakes at first" in the initial development of a performance indicator system, the "adoption of crude performance measures" and their refinement into the ultimate indicator system are the goals (Osborne and Gaebler 1993, p. 156). "Often simple is best, even if it initially seems less technically attractive" in developing indicators (Ewell and Jones 1994, p. 16). An indicator system must be flexible to permit evaluation of different kinds of institutions, using available data where possible to make the process more cost-effective. Multiple indicators are necessary to capture adequately the complexity of institutional performance. Finally, the designers of the system must remember that indicators are simply that—*indicators* of success, not precise measurements—and must be continuously improved to approximate a stated goal.

> *"Often simple is best, even if it initially seems less technically attractive" in developing indicators.*

Indeed, indicators as a system are best used to check a unit's health and progress. These systems, when combined with other efforts like accreditation, program review, and peer review can become a respected form of monitoring quality. A good performance indicator system can best be used as one of many instruments to monitor quality assurance, enhancement, and effectiveness. But performance indicator models have additional uses beyond this role.

The Use of Performance Indicators
It is appropriate at this point to discuss in more detail the uses and shortcomings of performance indicators. This discussion proposes a set of principles that are essential in the design

and implementation of effective performance indicators and points to some of the uses, benefits, and burdens that can be derived from that effort.

The definition of performance indicators includes several descriptors: effectiveness, efficiency, inputs, process, outputs, excellence, quality, accountability, and others. Indicators are:

> . . . *a concrete piece of information about a condition or result of public action that is regularly produced, publicly reported, and systematically used for planning, monitoring, or resource allocation at the state or system level. . . . [They are] intended to be used together, not singly or out of context* (Ewell and Jones 1994, p. 7).

> . . . *an authoritative measure—usually in quantitative form* . . . (Cave, Hanney, and Kogan 1991, p. 24).

> . . . *ratios, percentages, or other quantitative values that allow an institution to compare its position in key strategic areas to peers, to past performance, or to previously set goals* (Taylor, Meyerson, and Massy 1993, p. x).

These definitions correctly emphasize *performance,* but another theme that frequently occurs in definitions or discussions of performance indicators is the *quantitative* nature of the descriptors. The use of such data, however, suggests a precision of measurement that is often unattainable; as the label suggests, they are *indicators* of performance, "signals or guides rather than absolute measures" (Sizer, Spee, and Bormans 1992, p. 135). Thus, multiple indicators are necessary to produce a more accurate picture of an institution's overall operation, but *valid* and *reliable* indicators are also necessary. Bad data are worse than no data when indicators become the primary tool for managing higher education or allocating resources.

Performance indicators have five primary uses: monitoring, evaluation, dialogue, rationalization, and allocation of resources (Sizer, Spee, and Bormans 1992).

1. *Monitoring.* A study of quantitative management approaches to higher education nearly two decades ago noted that "the paramount need" was for "a standardized and consistent quantitative language" to monitor the use

of such techniques (Lawrence and Service 1977, pp. 15, 25). That language has now largely been established and the technology developed so that data, such as multiple performance indicators, can be collected and combined to characterize a particular institutional environment. Such efforts highly depend on the existence of information systems that, in turn, should dovetail with decision making and the institution's or system's responsibilities. The presence of accurate and reliable data now allows the monitoring of developments in a system, state, or nation.

2. *Evaluation.* Evaluation focuses on the attainment of goals, and objectives are normally quantifiable to enhance or facilitate such measurement. Multiple multidimensional indicators are necessary, even for the formative evaluation of an institution (Bogue and Saunders 1992); in their totality, such indicators would help provide a rational basis for decision making about progress toward or attainment of goals.

3. *Dialogue.* Using indicator systems, two or more parties are able to communicate with each other, attaching the same meaning to abstract concepts. The problems inherent in the lack of a standardized language have largely been solved through such agencies as the Organization for Economic Cooperation and Development (OECD) and the National Center for Education Statistics (NCES). And using indicators as a point of reference allows judgments, comparisons, and communication about the educational objectives of an institution, a state, a country, or a continent.

4. *Rationalization.* Rationalization is the accomplishment of a coherent policy-making process. Performance indicators can play a crucial role in planning, but an effective planning process must be in place before the application of indicators so that the accomplishment of policy can be measured.

5. *The allocation of resources.* Performance indicators can be used in the allocation of resources, but their validity should be high to prevent any unwanted or undesirable side effects, such as providing funding for indicators that do not measure what they purport to measure. Because some U.S. indicator systems sometimes lack validity and reliability, setting norms for comparison can be time-consuming.

The use of performance indicators ultimately involves comparisons—against oneself, a norm, or others. The use of such explicit comparisons, absent of judgment, emphatically means the identification of institutions or systems as above or below par. Labeling someone or something a "winner" or "loser," perhaps indirectly or unintentionally, is apt to occur, and university personnel, particularly faculty, voice considerable apprehension about a system that employs such summative judgments openly in, say, legislative hearings or state coordinating board meetings. Further, when such indicator systems are considered for redistribution of existing resources rather than the addition of resources, the results can also be negative and intimidating. "When organizations face conditions they define as threatening, the tendency is to become rigid—. . . centralized, conservative, protective, inflexible, and nonadaptable"—with the result often "a short-term, threat-induced crisis mentality" and the likelihood that organizational performance will suffer (Cameron and Tschirhart 1992, p. 88). The potential for damage with such a system is thus implicit, and some legitimate concerns have arisen that focus on the use of indicators and the ways in which individuals should be participating in their negotiation and development. If anything is to be accomplished in higher education, "it is going to be done by the professors or it is not going to be done at all" (Rudolph 1984, p. 13). It follows that any successful, sustained use of performance indicators in teaching or learning in U.S. higher education must involve faculty in the preparation and use of the system and in its reward mechanisms. Further, the careful development of such systems is crucial because of the potential for irrevocable damage (or improvement) they offer the organization (Blank 1993).

But just how easy is it to develop and implement a performance indicator system that actually works? If the experience of the U.S. business sector is indicative, the answer is "not very." Total quality management, benchmarking, reengineering, empowerment of the individual, and other current remedies are being proposed to unshackle U.S. workers and allow their creative juices to flow. But "no empirical evidence [shows] that any of these things [increase] productivity" (Bleakley 1993; see also Garver and Lucore 1993).

This conclusion should prod public policy makers to reflect on what their methods, including performance indicators, are doing to spur—or stifle—creativity, initiative, and learning.

These three items should be the goals of the remedies legislatures and coordinating boards are using to breathe new effectiveness, efficiency, and productivity into their higher education systems.

Since the 1950s, conventional employee management theory has held that people are motivated by the intrinsic satisfaction of a job: the opportunity for achievement, challenge, contributions, excitement, and personal recognition. But the basic structure of state incentive funding systems—like, for example, the Tennessee Performance Funding Program to improve instruction, the now-defunct New Jersey Challenge and Competitive Grants Program, Ohio's Selective Excellence Program, and Colorado's Incentive Financing Program—rewards and recognizes group or institutional incentives, often using institutional performance indicators to measure results before producing such rewards. Do such "collective rewards" effectively motivate individual faculty and students to achieve creativity, initiative, and learning? The answer to this question is not yet known or currently available in the literature.

If the idea, for example, is to encourage individual faculty to be entrepreneurial as a way to help fulfill a state's economic goals or to provide better-quality undergraduate education, then *individual involvement* is necessary for such indicator or incentive programs to be successful. Rewards must address the wants and needs of the individual learner and producer rather than focus on a uniform reward or incentives for an entire organization (Diamond and Adam 1993). How the institution internally uses these group incentive rewards, once received, to motivate individual learning, creativity, and initiative is another necessary ingredient to implement a quality and instructional improvement program that works.

A system can produce "an innovative organization" (Toombs and Tierney 1991, p. 79). Financial incentives for summer supplements and necessary resources to investigate a particular effort, for example, are tangible recognitions by administrators of what is valued and what is rewarded. The use of "potent symbols" is valuable in bringing about such organizational change (p. 79). For example, a reduction in course load to develop an undergraduate seminar would suggest the importance of undergraduate instruction to faculty. And leaders' efforts to communicate in writing and verbalize their appreciation and approval (or disapproval) of some effort is an essential ingredient for bringing about organizational change. "A central theme of much of the literature on organizational change is that innovating organizations must be specifically designed to innovate" (p. 74). Clearly, designing a reward system that includes individual incentives encourages innovative behavior that is measurable.

While it is not easy to implement a quality and incentive program with performance indicators that actually work, a key is to develop a program based on incentives that are meaningful to individuals, not solely to an institution.

Any discussion of the introduction of performance indicators into higher education in the United States must first take into account several landmark pieces of international literature (see especially Kells 1993; see also Bottani and Delfau 1990 and Cuenin 1987). Other works (Cave, Hanney, and Kogan 1991; Kells 1992b), published roughly concurrently with several studies published in the United States, have altered the landscape on the subject, both domestically and internationally. Further, NCES is moving toward collecting and publishing, for the first time, indicators that will allow states in this country to compare state-level performance with members of OECD (National Center for Education 1994a). It seems inevitable that such reports in the future will move toward more comparisons of states and countries, just as the current thrust in this country compares institutions and state support for education in areas like faculty salaries and educational and general funding. While this volume concentrates on public four-year institutions, systems, and state efforts, many of the principles and techniques found in private and community colleges are also applicable to other institutions (see, e.g., American Association of Community 1994; Doucette and Hughes 1993; Sapp 1993; Sapp and Temares 1991).

The following paragraphs describe some initial attempts toward performance indicators in the United States.

The NACUBO benchmarking project
An initial effort to prepare performance indicators, designed to create a national data base on higher education, was developed by the National Association of College and University Business Officers (NACUBO) in collaboration with the accounting firm Coopers & Lybrand, which largely developed the project and compiled the data. The project's primary focus was on developing comparative costs for a variety of administrative and financial functions (see table 2) and creating a

set of national standards or indicators to allow participating higher education institutions to measure or compare their efficiency and productivity. A national "benchmarking" project to allow comparisons in 38 functional areas, it was expected to allow—or prod—institutions to adapt innovative cost-cutting techniques from other comparable universities whose performance is more efficient. Several benchmarks from industries and businesses outside higher education, such as airlines and communications companies, will also be included in the project's results.

TABLE 2

FUNCTIONAL AREAS IN NACUBO's NATIONAL BENCHMARKING PROJECT

Academic affairs	Intercollegiate athletics
Accounts payable	Intramural and recreational sports
Admissions	Legal affairs
Alumni relations	Library
Bookstore	Mail
Career planning and placement center	Multicampus system administration
Central budget department	Parking
Central stores	Payroll
Collections	Police/security
Development office	Purchasing
Environmental health and safety	Registrar
Facilities	Sponsored projects
Financial aid	Student accounts receivable/Student billing
Food services	
General accounting	Student affairs
Human resources: Benefits administration	Student counseling
	Student health services
Human resources: General	Student housing
Human resources: Hiring	Telecommunications
Information technology	Treasury: Cash management

Source: Massy and Meyerson 1994, p. 94.

NACUBO's and its participating institutions' approach is somewhat of a reversal of the traditional reasons for collecting such data—from using results to justify more dollars from states, donors, and students to using them to cut costs and focus on productivity (Blumenstyk 1993, p. A41; Massy and Meyerson 1994, p. 94). Traditionally, institutions have focused on inputs and costs, equating better quality with greater expenditures. In contrast, benchmarking focuses on outputs and the quality of services. If an institution improves its services as a result of such efforts, it is in a better position to respond to its critics and better endure the harsh glare of public scrutiny.

With an initial sample of 120 institutions, NACUBO's benchmarking project began in 1992–93 with a two-year trial. One of the project's severe limitations for nonparticipants is the lack of information on individual colleges, as a result of participants' sensitivity about results. Another limitation is the lack of benchmarks for academic departments, although their inclusion is now being considered.

The Peterson's/AGB strategic indicators survey

This effort, like NACUBO's project, is designed to provide benchmarking for performance assessment. The project began in 1991 and subsequently was published by the Association of Governing Boards of Universities and Colleges (AGB) in two books on strategic indicators (Taylor, Meyerson, and Massy 1993; Taylor et al. 1991). An earlier volume by the AGB (Frances et al. 1987) developed a system of indicators for trustees. That effort was subsequently expanded in a survey of over 700 colleges and universities to develop comparative institutional data (see table 3) that was published by Peterson's Guides in Princeton (Massy and Meyerson 1994). The survey was "the most comprehensive effort of its kind ever undertaken in higher education" (p. 47), and the authors intend to update it approximately every two years and to develop data on trends. Results are provided separately for public and private universities, with brief statements of significance and interpretation for each strategic indicator. To assist in making meaningful comparisons, the data are broken down according to two-year colleges, regional colleges and universities, and research and land grant universities.

The NCHEMS indicators of good practice project

This project, for the National Center for Higher Education Management Systems (NCHEMS) under the guidance of Dr. Peter Ewell, focuses on developing a range of "good practice indicators" in undergraduate education. As policy, it is tied to the federal effort to develop indicators for tracking progress on national education goals, particularly goal 5.5, which

TABLE 3

MAJOR HEADINGS IN THE PETERSON'S/AGB STRATEGIC INDICATORS SURVEY QUESTIONNAIRE

Financial Profile

Revenue

Tuition and fee income

Government appropriations

Government grants and contracts

Private gifts, grants, and contracts

Endowment support for operations (payout or yield)

Sales and services of educational activities

Sales and services of auxiliary enterprises

Sales and services of hospitals

Other sources

Independent operations

Total revenue

Current Expenditures by Function

Instruction (including departmental research)

Organized research

Public service

Academic support

Student services (excluding student aid awards)

Institutional support

Plant operation and maintenance

Expenditures on auxiliaries

Expenditures on hospitals

Expenditures on independent operations

Student financial aid

Total expenditures

Current Expenditures by Object

Wages and salaries (by type of employee)

Fringe benefits

Interest payments to outside entities

Balance Sheet: Assets

Current funds

Endowment book value

Plant and equipment

Other assets

Total assets

Balance Sheet: Liabilities and Fund Balances

Current liabilities

Short-term debt to outside entities

Long-term debt to outside entities

Fund balances

Total liabilities and fund balances

Physical Plant Detail

Financial

  Beginning-of-year value

  Depreciation for the year

  Retirement of plant

  Additions to plant (new construction)

  End-of-year value

Plant inventory and condition

  Gross square feet (by type of facility)

Estimated deferred maintenance backlog ($)

Libraries and Information Resources Detail

Library holdings

  Book and monograph volumes

  Journal subscriptions

Information resources

  Microcomputers supplied for students' use

Endowment Detail

Beginning-of-year market value (by fund type)

Return on investment (by type of return)

Other additions to endowment (by type)

Subtractions from endowment

  Normal support for operations

  Special uses (e.g., to cover deficits)

  Total

End-of-year market value (by fund type)

Students

Fall enrollment (head count & FTE, by level)

Fall FTE enrollment by EEOC category and level

Fall FTE enrollment by gender and level

Fall FTE enrollment by field of study and level

Degrees awarded by level

Admissions data for the full year

  Number of applications

  Number of offers of admission

  Number of matriculants

  Geographic dispersion of entering students by level

  Number of states represented

  Student head count from home state

  Students from outside the U.S. and Canada

Tuition and financial aid

  Published charges

  Financial aid head counts by type of aid

  Financial aid dollars by type of aid

Faculty and Staff

Faculty numbers (full and part time, by rank)

Regular faculty FTE

  By field and rank

  By EEOC category and rank

  By gender and rank

  Percent faculty over 60 years old

Faculty gains and losses for the year by rank

  Head count at the beginning of the year

  In-hire

  Voluntary termination

  Termination by death or disability

  Termination by the institution

  Change category (e.g., nontenured to tenured)

  Head count at the end of the year

Sponsored Research

Expenditures for organized research

  U.S. government (direct and indirect, by major agency)

TABLE 3 (continued)

MAJOR HEADINGS IN THE PETERSON'S/AGB STRATEGIC
INDICATORS SURVEY QUESTIONNAIRE

State and local govt. agencies
Domestic corporations & corporate
   foundations
Other domestic private
   foundations
Foreign governments, corpo-
   rations, foundations
Bequests and gifts from living
   individuals
Other outside sponsors
Institutional funds
Academic-year faculty salary offsets

Percent of regular faculty members
   who are principal investigators
   on sponsored projects
Research proposal and award statistics
   Proposals sent to potential outside
      sponsors
   Awards received from outside
      sponsors

**Fundraising (Other than for
Sponsored Projects)**
Dollars raised during the year by
   source

Dollars raised during the year by
   use
   Designated or restricted for current
      operations
   Designated or restricted for student
      financial aid
   Designated or restricted for
      endowment
   Designated or restricted for plant
Percent of living alumni who are
   active donors (e.g., have given
   during the last five years

Note: The authors plan to offer the data on a subscription basis, which would allow institutional participants to compare their own data, variable by variable, with a selected profile of institutions and elements. Like the NACUBO study, research universities are underrepresented in the current data set, but this survey has more indicators on faculty and students than NACUBO's project.

Source: Massy and Meyerson 1994, pp. 48–49.

focuses on the ability of graduating college seniors to "think critically, communicate effectively, and solve problems" (National Center for Education 1994b). A feasibility study developed in fall 1993 focuses on three specific informational domains: institutional requirements, instructional practices, and student behaviors (Ewell 1993b; National Center for Education 1994b).

NCHEMS is working with a number of institutions to design systems of good practice indicators (see table 4). Approximately 60 different items can be identified and collected through a variety of methods of gathering data. Such information can be used to provide a regular benchmark for assessing collective progress in undergraduate education. Like earlier indicator projects, including the SUNY system's effort, such information about an institution can communicate concrete results easily and succinctly to parents and legislators on what kinds of experiences their children and constituents will encounter at a particular college or university (see Ewell 1994c; National Center for Education 1994b; National Center for Higher 1993b).

TABLE 4

**HEADINGS FOR THE NCHEMS INDICATORS
OF GOOD PRACTICE PROJECT**

Institutional context and use of resources
Curriculum/class structure and requirements
Teaching practice and the classroom environment
Student behavior and the campus environment
Term registration records
Transcript studies of graduating seniors
End-of-course course evaluation survey items
Faculty surveys
Student surveys
Periodic course syllabus studies
Periodic studies of the library and other academic support areas

Sources: Ewell 1993b; National Center for Education 1994b.

The ECS project

With a 1992 grant from the Fund for the Improvement of Post-secondary Education (FIPSE), the Education Commission of the States (ECS) is conducting a ten-state study to furnish public policy makers with a set of indicators useful for monitoring the educational quality of state systems of higher education, and for improving teaching and learning on campus. The ten states included in the study—Colorado, Florida, Illinois, Kentucky, New York, South Carolina, Tennessee, Texas, Virginia, and Wisconsin—were selected because of their existing indicator systems or their efforts to develop an indicator system. The objectives for this project link the search for education indicators to concepts of what quality means as an aspect of teaching and learning for states, systems, or campuses. With such a diverse group of representative states, the ECS project attempts to start the discussion with a concept of quality and its implications for a set of performance standards and expectations for higher education as a whole. From there, it is reviewing the efforts of the pilot states and developing a conceptual framework for assessing state or system performance as it serves the needs of various constituencies—the state, the public, and students. A number of publications on performance indicators are being developed as a result of this project, including a report on each state and several related publications on performance indicators and undergraduate education (see, in particular, Ruppert 1994e).

Patterns of Performance Indicators for the 1990s

The development of performance indicators in the 1990s differs from that in the 1980s. The 1980s went through a number of evolutionary stages, but the continuing focus of policy was on quality, undergraduate education, and productivity, among others. Several distinct new patterns have emerged in the 1990s, however (see, in particular, Ewell 1994a).

A concern with both quality and efficiency

The concern with quality continues to capture the attention of policy makers in the 1990s, but this theme now coincides with states' greater interest in economic development and the emergence of higher education's second recession in the past ten years (Blumenstyk and Cage 1991; Minter 1992, p. 26). As colleges and universities began to recover from the economic slump in 1987, economic decline began again in FY 1990, with public four-year colleges and universities experiencing the sharpest decline in growth of educational and general budgets. Total state appropriations to higher education in FY 1992, in absolute terms, were smaller than in the preceding year, and appropriations in FY 1993 failed to keep pace with inflation in three-fourths of the states (Folger and Jones 1993, p. 5). Although early projections were that this decline would be even deeper than the 1987 recession, the recession appeared to ameliorate in 1994 (Cage 1994, p. A19). At the same time, skepticism among state and federal taxpayers about what they are getting from universities for their tax dollars has caused a growing legislative interest in efficiency and productivity, particularly in faculty workloads, which has become linked with the continuing concern about quality ("Universities Grapple" 1994). The most immediate result of this pattern was a greater link between planning and budget allocations; in Texas, for example, House Bill 2009 (1991) and Senate Bill 1332 (1993) required state plans for all state agencies, including higher education. In their requests for appropriations to the legislature, Texas higher education agencies were required to link their plan, its stated goals, and the related fiscal request as a way of better connecting fiscal accountability with promised results.

Quick implementation with little prior conceptual development

By 1994, some 18 states had a performance indicator system in place, the majority of them developed and implemented in the previous three years. Legislation by fax prevailed, with imitation frequently copying poor-quality indicators from one state to another (although some good features also were copied). On the positive side, this pattern suggests awareness of common problems and a quick response from legislators by using the same solutions.

More deliberate links between planning/ resources and indicator systems

The 1980s witnessed few major successful state policy efforts linking planning and budgeting. Indeed, considerable evidence in the literature successfully linking planning and budgeting has not proved effective in practice, despite the sanctity in its belief as an article of faith (Schmidtlein 1989–90). A notable exception is the case of Tennessee and its highly published experiment with performance funding (Banta 1988; Marchese 1985). Texas also toyed with the idea of performance funding, but the legislature has yet to adopt the system (Ashworth 1994; Bateman and Elliott 1994; Gaither 1993). Despite the "renaissance," however, the "political reality may prohibit its full implementation, [as] performance budgeting tends to have little 'pork barrel appeal'" (Lasher and Greene 1993, p. 448).

A critical question is whether such funds will be taken from base funding or be added as supplementary funding.

While performance funding, along with the national movement to reinvent government and transform the public sector (Osborne and Gaebler 1993), is witnessing something of a "renaissance," performance budgeting paradoxically had its beginnings in another reform period—the Progressive Era—in New York City during the mid-1910s (Mikesell 1982, p. 83). It again surfaced in the late 1940s during the second major stage of the formation of public administration and planning (Meisinger and Dubeck 1984, p. 185). In all three periods, the budget was viewed as an instrument to control expenditures, with the intent of improving efficiency.

It is unclear whether performance funding will be the fiscal lever to accompany the current reform movement, but some type of incentive funding appears to be destined for connection with state performance indicator systems in the 1990s. A critical question is whether such funds will be taken from base funding or be added as supplementary funding.

The deliberate concentration on comparisons of institutional performance in current performance indicator systems

The 1980s found legislatures and state higher education boards reluctant to press for institutional comparisons; instead, they emphasized institutions' *voluntary* improvement. Institutions were given the opportunity to make improvements voluntarily (Aper, Cuver, and Hinkle 1990), but by the 1990s policy makers' patience was wearing thin with institutions' perceived foot-dragging and a more forceful pattern of required comparisons is emerging.

Policy makers' greater resistance to institutional pressure

The 1980s found legislators more willing to compromise concerning proposed requirements for indicator systems, but the 1990s find greater resistance to institutional protests about such matters. Several state educational systems—New York, Virginia, and Wisconsin, in particular—have engaged in preemptive strikes. Perhaps sensing the inevitability of stronger accountability and performance systems, these states and systems of higher education took the initiative and developed (or are developing) systems of performance indicators on their own (often requiring significant statistical and data collection) to demonstrate to the public and to policy makers their willingness to comply with requirements for accountability. The University of Wisconsin system, for example, is working with its state government to develop better measures of accountability. The governor established the Accountability Task Force, which included university representatives, in March 1993 to identify specific indicators to measure the university system's performance in seven areas: quality, effectiveness, efficiency, access, diversity, stewardship of assets, and contribution to compelling state needs (see table 5). Core indicators were developed, and each institution also developed measures of accountability. Performance will be reported on a regular basis. To date, the response to the effort has been positive, helping communicate to policy makers and

TABLE 5

SOME ACCOUNTABILITY INDICATORS FROM THE UNIVERSITY OF WISCONSIN SYSTEM'S ACCOUNTABILITY FOR ACHIEVEMENT PROGRAM

Quality
- Student satisfaction surveys regarding accessibility of faculty inside and outside the classroom; quality of instruction; academic and career advising; course availability; involvement in faculty-based research; institutional responsiveness to students' concerns, etc.
- Alumni satisfaction surveys conducted five years after graduation regarding their assessment of the quality of education received with respect to career preparation, involvement in civic, cultural affairs, community service, and cultural achievement
- Percentage of all undergraduate course enrollments and instructor hours taught by instructor type—faculty, instructional academic staff, and teaching assistants

Effectiveness
- Results of systemwide sophomore competency tests (ACT–CAAP) or other Board-approved alternative tests
- Graduation rate of undergraduates by full- and part-time status
- GRE, LSAT, and test scores of students, job placement rates, professional and graduate school acceptance rates, pass rates on licensure exams, and other data showing postgraduate experience and success

Efficiency
- Average credits to degree for students graduating with a B.A.; proportion of students graduating in four years, by residency
- Proportion of payrolled FTE positions and expenditures accounted for by institutional support, academic support, instruction, and student services

Access
- Percentage of qualified undergraduate resident students accepted for admission; percentage of Wisconsin high school students who enroll immediately in the UWS

Diversity
- Progress toward EEO/AA goals in hiring, promotion, and tenure of women and minority faculty and staff
- Number and residency of minority students by race and ethnicity; graduation rates of same
- Incidents of sexual harassment

Stewardship of Assets
- Recruitment and retention rates of faculty and expenditures on faculty and staff development

TABLE 5 (continued)

SOME ACCOUNTABILITY INDICATORS FROM THE UNIVERSITY OF WISCONSIN SYSTEM'S ACCOUNTABILITY FOR ACHIEVEMENT PROGRAM

- Progress on addressing preventative maintenance needs of university facilities
- Number and severity of accidents, injuries, and identified losses or safety risks

Contribution to Compelling State Needs
- Results of employer surveys regarding their assessment of the career preparation of UWS graduates, their satisfaction with the responsiveness of the UWS to their needs for technical assistance and other outreach services
- Enrollments in continuing education programs, including a demographic analysis of participants and an analysis of users' perspectives on emerging needs and unmet demand

Note: For more detail, see University of Wisconsin System 1994.

the public alike that the university system is being accountable to the state ("Strengthening" 1994, p. 3). Perhaps the most successful and most publicized of these preemptive strikes to date, however, has been SUNY's effort (see, e.g., Burke 1993b; Richardson 1994f, p. 65).

The K–12 connection
A current question of policy in developing performance indicators is the tendency to connect reform in kindergarten through grade 12 (K–12) with reform in higher education (Ewell 1994a). Policy makers perceive that reform in kindergarten through grade 12 is working and that all public education should therefore be integrated and connected into a continuum, or public accountability framework. Thus, policy makers are thinking not in terms of K–12, but K–16. The state of Kentucky, which has thoroughly reformed its K–12 program in the 1990s, is the most prominent example of this manifestation (Ruppert 1994a, p. 52). The connection is present but less obvious in other states, and it appears the trend could exhibit itself more often in the 1990s. National organizations representing the K–12 arena have been actively using blue ribbon committees to identify and define essential content

and standards for what students should know and be able to perform. The National Council of Teachers of Mathematics, for example, led the way when it released math standards in 1989. Standards in visual arts, music, theater, and dance, and standards in geography were released in 1994, and as of late 1994 more national standards in history, civics, and government were being developed. Federal legislation promotes the use of national standards or indicators in kindergarten through grade 12. The "Goals 2000: Educate America Act," signed into law in March 1993, encourages states to set such standards but does not yet tie funding to the use of national standards. These various standards provide visible resources and models to draw upon as state policy makers review their educational enterprises. Nowhere, it appears, are state policy makers adopting the standards wholesale, so the long-term connection could be less dramatic than some proponents had hoped for.

Summary

A caveat should be noted here concerning the number of variations among states within these major policy themes of the 1990s. The states' history of public policy is manifestly different according to individual state's actions (Bogue 1993). Georgia's legislature, for example, in recent years has provided significant independence to its higher education system and has produced no major legislative acts concerning accountability, quality, or required performance reporting (Bogue, Creech, and Folger 1993). In contrast, the state of Florida has a history of mandating academic program reviews, outcomes for general education (e.g., the College-Level Academic Skills Test), selected indices of productivity, and annual reports on a number of state-level performance indicators (Florida State 1992; Van de Water 1994b, p. 27). The political party in power, personalities, the public mood, the quality of leadership, state economic conditions, and other factors can drive or accentuate differences in states' responses. But despite the tendency to copy indicators from one state to another, many states clearly have taken a proactive approach, emphasizing one or more initiatives to promote or achieve quality assurance. The following subsection reviews some of the approaches various states are emphasizing to achieve public accountability and quality assurance.

Responding to the Challenge of Public Accountability

The Government [is] very keen on amassing statistics—they collect them, add them, raise them to the nth power, take the cube root, and prepare wonderful diagrams. But what you must never forget is that every one of those figures comes in the first instance from the chowty dar [the Indian village watchman], who just puts down what he damn pleases.

—Josiah Stamp (1929)

The 1990s clearly are witnessing a change in policy makers' attitudes toward higher education. The general tone is one of less voluntary institutional improvement and more mandated public accountability. For example, of ten "front-burner issues" for colleges and universities, "oversight and accountability" was one of the first identified (Association of Governing 1994). The AGB predicts that the federal government will become "more directly involved in the review of institutions" and that "increased skepticism about accreditation" will see new state agencies involved in the fiscal, academic, and administrative review of institutions (1994).

Accreditation agencies were once regarded as trusted gatekeepers of quality. Now, however, they are being viewed, particularly at the federal level, with suspicion and as a series of old boy networks in which hardly anyone ever fails or is held fully accountable. The new state agencies predicted by AGB probably will serve more to monitor and enforce increasing federal laws or regulations. Some standards, such as those recently developed for state postsecondary review entities (SPREs), are becoming de facto federal performance standards, which will be monitored by individual states. Clear losers in this shift of power are the accreditation agencies. Some accreditation agencies, such as the Southern Association of Colleges and Schools, the North Central Association, and the Middle States Association, are responding to federal concerns, but most such agencies still appear recalcitrant. Thus, a theme of more centralized authority to bring about more public accountability and better management, particularly at the state level, will likely underlie the ways that many of higher education's future funding needs will be addressed.

Partially as a result of this climate, current funding mechanisms for higher education must change to focus on educational goals rather than continuing to promote mostly equity in funding and access as they have for the last 20 years (Albright 1994). Higher education must now "move to a value-driven system [that] focuses on student and institutional performance and improvements" (pp. 7, 8).

This emphasis on "a clean slate" for funding in the 1990s is another example of the way some current policy makers are actively seeking to provide more public accountability and institutional improvement. In the 1980s, colleges and universities were encouraged to develop *voluntary* improvements, particularly in undergraduate education, and document what results were achieved (Aper, Cuver, and Hinkle 1990). Now, however, public accountability, using fiscal policy and state legislation, has become a central purpose of states' efforts rather than a voluntary by-product.

Other new approaches to funding would promote greater improvement in performance and greater public accountability, thereby encouraging the use of performance indicators. The Texas Commissioner of Higher Education, for example, believing that such systems will be used more frequently in the future, has developed a performance indicator system for possible use in Texas (see table 6) (Ashworth 1994). A fresh approach to state fiscal policy as applied to institutions of higher education is not necessarily designed to generate more funds than other fiscal policies, for decreased funding for higher education is not a temporary condition (Folger and Jones 1993). Instead, the proposed system is designed to ensure that states' interests and educational priorities are closely connected, almost symbiotically, during the allocation process. This three-part state budget system would include a base or core lump-sum budget, a capital budget, and a special-purpose budget (Folger and Jones 1993):

- *The core lump-sum budget.* Subject to an institution's accountability and assessment of its achieving its goals, the institution would be authorized to manage this budget, with a minimum of interference.
- *The capital budget.* This budget would cover the acquisition of assets and new buildings.
- *The special-purpose budget.* This budget, at 5 to 10 percent of the base budget, would be tied to the state's objectives; based on some form of assessment to measure progress, such as performance indicators, the monies would be

used to advance the state's agenda through its higher education system. (It is important that this budget be in addition to the base budget, not a portion of it. Otherwise, it is vulnerable to elimination at the first sign of a decreased budget [Hollander 1991].)

The special-purpose budget could assume several different forms during allocations:

TABLE 6

PROPOSED PERFORMANCE FUNDING RATES AND INDICATORS FOR TEXAS

	Weight	Units per Year	Dollars (1994)	Dollars (1995)	Rate (1994)	Rate (1995)
1. Undergraduate Degrees Awarded	10%	50,590	$ 6,134,478	$ 12,424,842	$121.26	$ 245.60
2. Semester Credit Hours Completed	10%	7,746,836	6,134,478	12,424,842	0.79	1.60
3. Success of Students Needing Remediation	10%	6,347	6,134,478	12,424,842	966.52	1,957.59
4. Minority Graduates	10%	10,836	6,134,478	12,424,842	566.12	1,146.63
5. Community College Transfers Who Graduate	10%	12,275	6,134,478	12,424,842	499.75	1,012.21
6. Lower-Division Classes Taught by Tenured or Tenure-Track Faculty	10%	10,444	6,134,478	12,424,842	587.37	1,189.66
7. Externally Funded Research	10%	332,258,701	6,134,478	12,424,842	0.02	0.04
8. Minority Students Enrolled	20%	97,273	12,268,956	24,849,684	126.13	255.46
9. Community College Transfer Students Enrolled	10%	65,739	6,134,478	12,424,842	93.32	189.00
TOTAL	100%		$61,344,780	$124,248,420		

Note: The House proposal was for $61.3 million, the Senate proposal for $20 million. Estimated for illustration.

- *Block grants.* Perhaps the best example of such an effort is Ohio's Selective Excellence Program, which existed from 1983 to 1991. One part of this six-part program was the "academic challenge" block grant, which awarded $86 million from 1985 to 1991. Institutions used the block grants, which amounted to 1 percent of the state's appropriations, to strengthen their strong programs and develop additional centers of excellence (Folger and Jones 1993, p. 36; National Center for Higher 1992).
- *Initiative or prospective (competitive) funding.* Virginia has provided competitive grants since 1980, and New Jersey, using a base-plus budget enhancement model from 1984 to 1990, had a dozen such programs and awarded

over $50 million (although it eliminated all competitive programs in 1990–91, primarily as a result of budget cuts and institutional opposition). State objectives, such as increasing the retention and graduation rates of minorities, are normally funded under such competitive grants, and institutions can use the funds in some entrepreneurial way of their choosing to achieve the state's objectives. Because such state objectives have lower priorities with institutions than their base budgets and core objectives, when funds are decreased, institutions seek to preserve the basics first (Hollander 1991; Morgan 1992, p. 290).

• *Incentive funding.* Such grants are awarded on the basis of progress toward a state goal. Typically, a state develops performance indicators of undergraduate quality and effectiveness and provides "incentive funding" for an institution that achieves or exceeds some designated standard. Colorado, for example, passed an incentive financing law in 1993 to strengthen undergraduate education and to increase historically bypassed student populations (Lively 1994). Tennessee's performance funding (instructional improvement) project, which began in 1979, allowed each institution to earn up to 2 percent of its state appropriations. More complex rules were added to Tennessee's program in the 1980s, primarily to ensure fairness and reduce game playing (Folger and Jones 1993, p. 37; Morgan 1992, p. 292).

• *Student funding (scholarships and work-study grants).* A commonly used practice to enhance and enrich undergraduate education, financial aid and state scholarships are used to attract and help retain star (high-achieving) students. Another approach is to use them to attract a different mix of students. Texas, for example, through special funding provides scholarships to white students to attend a historically black college in the state. In a related vein, Missouri provides a designated amount of funding to an institution for each minority graduate under its "Funding for Results" program.

Such proposals suggest that traditional funding systems in higher education could contain serious disincentives that discourage a faculty member's commitment to teaching or meeting state goals. Clearly, the internal reward system seems at odds with state goals on improving and enriching undergraduate education. On university campuses, for example, the primary and coveted rewards for faculty are more merit pay, promotion, tenure, teaching graduate students, research, and publication—not necessarily in that order (see, in particular, Diamond and Adam 1993). At the state level, some commonly stated goals for higher education over the last decade include better and more innovative undergraduate instruction involving senior faculty, more public accountability (and, thus, often more control over the campus), achievement of collective, particularly economic, goals for the state, better health care services, and greater access for historically underserved populations, who often require remedial or developmental education. Clearly, the conflicting general objectives of both parties carry within them some friction and dissonance. The state wields the budget ax and the legislature to stimulate faculty, but the faculty can employ passive resistance. The use of fiscal policy and incentives as outlined earlier with valid and reliable performance indicators to measure and reward progress could foster new vision and innovation in college teaching. A new approach using fiscal policy could provide the stimulus needed to create an increasingly homogenous set of goals for both institutions and society. Faculty have yet to respond with commitment to such externally imposed accountability systems (Burke 1994, p. 3).

Although performance indicators for higher education became established in Europe in the 1980s, these activities are still relatively new in the United States. Before such indicators can be effectively employed to ensure better public accountability, it will be necessary first for the states, in conjunction with the education community, to adopt clear goals or expectations for their higher education systems. If a higher education system's goals are not known and are not clear, then how can a set of performance indicators be adequately applied to measure, evaluate, and reward progress toward desired goals?

The ongoing ten-state project by the Education Commission of the States has identified certain general areas around which state goals and expectations are developing: effectiveness, efficiency/productivity, access, quality of undergraduate education, equity/diversity, state economic development needs, and contributions to reform of elementary and secondary education (Ruppert 1994e). The fact that these ten states have focused on common topics for the improvement of performance is further evidence that a core set of common problems probably exists across the states. A state must delineate clear, measurable goals before a performance indicator system can be used to maximum benefit.

Performance indicators, used now in some 18 states, with some exceptions contain 15 to 20 distinct items for collecting data (Ewell 1994b, p. 16). The following list includes the common core of performance indicators identified by the ten states in the ECS project:

- Enrollment/graduation data by gender, ethnicity, and program
- Degree completions and time to degree
- Persistence/retention rates by grade, ethnicity, and program
- Number/percent of accredited eligible programs
- Remediation activities and indicators of their effectiveness
- Transfer rates to and from two- and four-year institutions
- Pass rates on professional exams (e.g., CPA, nursing, engineering)
- Job placement data on graduates and graduates' satisfaction with their jobs
- Faculty workload and productivity in the form of student/faculty ratios and instructional contact hours.

Other lists, however (see, e.g., Taylor, Meyerson, and Massy 1993), include entirely different indicators (see table 7). While the indicators shown on table 7 are "critical success factors" for an institution, the differences in lists further signify the conflict between state and institutional definitions of "success" (see, in particular, Cave, Hanney, and Kogan 1991, p. 153). Further, it is difficult, at the state level, to use state fiscal policy and performance indicators to measure the achievement of any agreed-upon state educational goals, although such differences can be resolved (Richardson 1994a, p. 131).

While these ECS core indicators are commonly used, several states have added embellishments that distinguish them from the norm. South Carolina, for example, collects information on upper-division students' involvement in sponsored research. Virginia collects information on undergraduate students' integrative experiences. A number of states have indicators regarding small classes (Wisconsin and Virginia) or class size by level (New York) in line with the commonly held belief that small classes have a high positive value for improving the quality of undergraduate education—even though the idea is not necessarily supported by research (Williams et al. 1985). Such indicators based on class size could represent another area where the validity of some existing state performance measures can be called into question.

The *core* list of performance indicators in the United States is comparable to indicators used in other countries (see Borden and Banta 1994; Bottrill and Borden 1994, p. 107; Cave, Hanney, and Kogan 1991, p. 172; Cuenin 1987, p. 135;

TABLE 7

TOP TEN "CORE" INDICATORS

1. Overall Revenue Structure
2. Overall Expenditure Structure
3. Excess (Deficit) or Current Fund Revenues over (or under) Current Fund Expenditures
4. Percent of Freshman Applicants Accepted and Percent of Accepted Freshman Who Matriculate
5. Ratio of Full-Time Equivalent Students to Full-Time Equivalent Faculty
6. Institutional Grant Aid as a Percent of Tuition and Fee Income
7. Tenure Status of Full-Time Equivalent Faculty
8. Percent of Total Full-Time Equivalent Employees Who Are Faculty
9. Maintenance Backlog as a Percent of Total Replacement Value of Plant
10. Percent of Living Alumni Who Have Given at Any Time during the Past Five Years

Source: Taylor, Meyerson, and Massy 1993, pp. xv–xvi.

Sizer, Spee, and Bormans 1992, p. 151), although in some cases the terminology differs. The British, for example, refer to attrition and persistence rates as "wastage" and first job placement as "first destination" (Cave, Hanney, and Kogan 1991, p. 95). On the other hand, citation indices (e.g., number of publications cited in works) and research produced are common international performance indicators that are used infrequently in the United States (see, e.g., Cave, Hanney, and Kogan 1991, p. 114; Hattie 1990). Instead, for example, Colorado's House Bill 1187, in effect from 1985 to 1991, mandating accountability in Colorado in higher education, and Colorado's 1993 "incentive financing" law emphasize strengthening undergraduate education and reaching students who would not normally go to college (Frantz 1992; Lively 1994; Van de Water 1994a). Indeed, a distinct difference between European and U.S. performance indicators is that the U.S. version does not adequately recognize or reward graduate or professional training, or research. Further, the focus on economic development and job placement data about graduates in some of the core U.S. indicator systems makes land grant and professional institutions better able to benefit or comply with such indicators than liberal arts institutions or predominantly graduate and research institutions.

Summary

Higher education in the United States in the 1990s has witnessed the emergence or reshaping of several trends. First, policy makers' mood has changed since the 1980s, when legislatures seemed more willing to compromise with institutions, to a harder line, often manifesting itself now through the legislative process. This trend was fueled by a decided shift in the 1990s to more demands for greater public accountability and accompanied by a shift in sentiment that saw 18 states' rather rapid adoption of performance indicators, most during the first three years of the decade. These adaptations were often accomplished through imitation—with all of the flaws and virtues transmitted from one state to another.

Accompanying these trends were responses by several professional organizations or institutes—NACUBO, NCHEMS, AGB, and others—to develop indicators. Many of these efforts are designed to identify and define a set of performance indicators and develop normative data that will allow for comparisons among institutions.

The states involved in designing performance indicators share common problems (and goals) with their higher education systems. A core set of common performance indicators began to evolve around these problems, cutting across a number of states and showing similarities with international efforts. A major difference, however, is that U.S. indicators tend to focus on undergraduate education or economic development more than their overseas counterparts.

Several new approaches to budgeting have been proposed that support the growing trend in the United States toward greater public accountability. Incentives to support or buttress state formula funding were developed. Focusing more on process, outputs, and the quality of the efforts, such outcomes-

Several new approaches to budgeting have been proposed that support the growing trend in the United States toward greater public accountability.

oriented efforts were designed to provide incentives to accomplish desired goals.

Accompanying these efforts are questions, still unanswered, about the use of group incentives to bring about institutional change. Reform must begin with the individual—more specifically in higher education, with the faculty's support—for it to be effective. And how much is money, when dispensed to an institution rather than an individual, a motivator to bring about needed reform? A certain tension between the campus and the state (or Washington, D.C.) appears on the horizon, particularly as greater centralization of decision making at the state level grows imminent. The goals of the faculty and the state legislature often appear at odds, almost guaranteeing some level of ongoing tension and conflict between these groups. The regional and national role of accrediting associations appears to be eroding, being replaced by, among others, the federal government in areas like financial aid and national performance goals. And the trend appears to be growing, with more centralization by the states following the "Republican revolution" during the 1994 elections.

The use of performance indicators does not stop at our shores. Indeed, Americans have gained a great deal of experience with the problems and issues that fueled these reforms elsewhere—particularly in Europe and Australia, the focus of the next section.

THE INTERNATIONAL USE OF PERFORMANCE INDICATORS

An examination of the use of performance indicators internationally reveals a wide range of philosophies and applications. Despite this diversity, the use of indicators generally occurs within a framework of increased government accountability and fiscal constraint, as governments' concept of their role in higher education shifted from a type of "public utility" to a "strategic investment" (Ewell 1991). Effective performance has become an integral part of the discussion overseas about excellence and quality, as it has in the United States. Consequently, international approaches to assessment and evaluation share a common connection to budgeting processes for state systems and individual institutions.

Background

At no time in its history has higher education been faced with greater demands to demonstrate its worth and account for its use of public resources (Kogan 1989). But a shift from professional self-evaluation to external and managerial assessment reveals a number of common problems:

1. The application of evaluation techniques used in industry, which are of limited value to higher education, especially those emphasizing outcomes or product rather than process.
2. The change in assessment criteria from those stressing excellence to criteria related to economic or social outcomes.
3. Questions of power regarding mechanisms, motivations, and methodologies for assessment.

Despite the considerable interest generated by discussions about performance indicators, indicators ostensibly play a relatively minor role in the actual policies and decisions of most governments and institutions. A number of factors limit the impact of performance indicators:

1. The connection between indicators and selective funding, viewed as threatening to institutions.
2. Issues of validity and reliability in the selection and application of performance indicators.
3. A lack of conceptual agreement between governments and institutions on the use of indicators (Sizer, Spee, and Bormans 1992).

Nevertheless, consensus is growing in Europe regarding the usefulness of performance indicators in reshaping education—particularly when they are complemented with more qualitative information (Jongbloed and Westerheijden 1994).

This section summarizes the literature on the use of performance indicators in selected countries outside the United States, compares indicator systems in use around the world, and summarizes the major themes presented in the profiles of systems used in other countries.

The Use of Performance Indicators

In light of the wide range of assumptions, approaches, intentions, and levels of sophistication present in performance indicators, some criteria are necessary to compare them so that their usefulness and replicability in other settings can be assessed. The following comparative criteria are used as the framework to describe performance indicator systems in Canada, Australia, and five countries in Europe and to show the links among organizational culture, institutional change, governmental and managerial priorities, and pedagogy:

1. Locus of control
2. Degree of government involvement
3. Focus of performance indicators
4. Sources of variation in quality
5. Data selection
6. Intended audiences
7. Emphasis of use
8. Impact on students' learning
9. Relationship to institutional mission (Nedwek and Neal 1994b).

These nine dimensions provide a framework for the examination of similarities and differences in the development of indicator systems in the selected countries, as well as a theoretical basis for the analysis of strengths and weaknesses in each initiative.

Locus of control

Change within higher education institutions results primarily from one of two sources: internal forces of reform or external demands from the environment. The organization is engaged in a struggle over control with its environment (Peterson and Spencer 1993), but because of higher education's dual system

of governance (administrators and professionals), the usefulness of traditional management techniques, such as strategic "control" mechanisms, is limited (De Jager 1992). Nevertheless, the mechanisms used for control in organizations
including higher education can be classified into clans,
bureaucracies, and markets (Ouchi 1989). Clans seek to control members' behavior through shared values, traditions, and
social structures, such as those found among faculty in departments, schools, or universities. Bureaucracies control through
hierarchical authority and rules, such as state agencies or
accrediting bodies. Markets rely on forces like competition
and pricing to shape organizational behavior.

Degree of government involvement
While government involvement can be viewed as a subset
of locus of control, it is distinct in this discussion because of
the interplay of perceptions between government officials
and academic leaders (Nedwek and Neal 1994b). The level
of government involvement is dictated by the scarcity of
resources and the attitudes, beliefs, and values within the political culture (Boyer 1990; Ewell 1989). These perceptions
in turn shape the form and substance of assessment systems.
Government involvement ranges from direct to indirect to
laissez-faire. Direct involvement results from state-mandated
systems with prescribed methodologies for the design and
use of performance indicators. Indirect control encourages
limited delegation of authority to institutions to accommodate
diversity within the context of broad goal statements. A
laissez-faire position exists when government leaders show
disinterest in educational policy or when coordinated efforts
are largely voluntary.

Focus of performance indicators
Performance indicators should be directly related to the institution's functions and goals (Ball and Wilkinson 1992; Dochy
and Segers 1990). The foci of indicators include effectiveness
(how well the institution accomplishes its stated goals and
objectives), increasing efficiency (what it costs to achieve
those goals), or improving the institution's economic environment (how to save money yet achieve the goals).

Sources of variation in quality
The philosophy of continuous and systematic improvement
stresses the importance of reducing variation in production

design and processes (Deming 1986). Special causes of variation (such as individual performance) must be kept analytically distinct from common causes (those attributable to poor institutional processes), for common causes (variations in design, materials, technologies, and supervision) will substantially affect the quality of an institution (Dill 1992). Special causes of variations are exceptions to the normal process that require quick detection and administrative action to eliminate (Chaffee and Sherr 1992). Analyses of common causes of variation often result in an overemphasis on the connection between inputs and outcomes, resulting in a call for increased assessment of the process as a component of institutional evaluation (Nedwek 1994; Schilling and Schilling 1993).

Data selection

In the absence of consensus on conceptual frameworks, the options for gathering and selecting data vary widely but usually reflect a classic mechanistic view of organizations. While some systems select data about input, processes, and outcomes to assess quality (Ball and Halwachi 1987; Chaffee and Sherr 1992; Scottish Higher Education 1992), most institutions still concentrate primarily on measures of input (Johnes and Taylor 1990). Methods of collecting data reflect a quantitative bias and tend to include such measures because they are readily available and easily quantifiable (Ball and Wilkinson 1992; Elton 1987). This quantitative bias is revealed in the development of proxy measures of process, such as human resource ratios (faculty/staff and faculty per FTE student, for example) (Schmitz 1993). In an era of fiscal constraint, financial ratio analysis has emerged as a way to assess financial performance, institutional priorities, and comparisons of peer organizations (Chabotar 1989; DiSalvo 1989; KPMG Peat Marwick 1990).

Intended audiences

Higher education institutions produce performance indicators for a variety of audiences, including governing bodies, legislatures, students, and faculty. The following typology categorizes these audiences by relationship to the institution and anticipated outcome of the information:
1. Internal decision makers (administration/faculty)
2. Internal policy makers (board/administration)
3. External decision makers (parents/students)

4. External policy makers (government agencies/accreditation bodies) (Nedwek and Neal 1994b).

Emphasis of use

Performance indicators have four primary purposes: (1) monitoring general conditions and contexts; (2) identifying progress toward specified goals; (3) illuminating or foreshadowing problems; and (4) diagnosing potential sources of identified problems (Darling-Hammond 1992). They can serve two additional purposes as well: the allocation of incentive funding and resources (Banta 1986; "Development of" 1985); and political symbolism (Ewell 1989; Kalsbeek 1991; Leviton and Hughes 1981; Nedwek and Neal 1994a; Weiss 1977).

Impact on students' learning

Most performance indicator systems reflect primarily responsiveness to external pressures and demands. As a result, little attention is given to processes within the organization, especially the learning environment (Nedwek and Neal 1994b). Sensitivity to process or the program's effects on students' learning can be direct, indirect, or assumed. Direct impact exists when the model intentionally yields data to validate students' achievement as related to the institution's mission. Indirect impact represents models that foster a concern about variations in outcomes and links to the delivery of programs. Assumed impact, the most common model, exists when student outcomes serve as a leap of faith from the program outline—for example, the connection between improvements in productivity and enhancement of academic quality (Massy and Wilger 1992).

Relationship to institutional mission

Performance indicators vary in the degree to which they are related to programmatic, institutional, or systemwide missions. While mission statements should provide a starting point in the development of indicators, the actual relationship might be direct, indirect, or assumed (Nedwek and Neal 1994b). A direct relationship exists when the mission statement clearly promotes the institution's distinctiveness, and such a statement should therefore include clear goals about intended outcomes, clientele to be served, and steps to ensure achievement of the mission (Bogue and Saunders 1992; Newsom and

Hayes 1990). An indirect relationship exists when the mission statement and the performance assessment system suggest less precise standards. Assumed relationships occur when mission statements and performance indicators are independent.

Case Studies
Great Britain
Background. Rapid increases in enrollment, the demand for the efficient use of resources, and the final abolition in 1992 of the binary educational system (two distinct sectors—polytechnic schools and colleges, and universities) have set the tone for significant changes in governance, funding, and allocations in Great Britain. Public institutions in Great Britain include 150 former polytechnic schools and colleges and 43 universities (excluding the Open University). Although the polytechnic schools still maintain a more vocational focus, some of the larger institutions have an academic reputation higher than the universities (Goedegebuure, Maassen, and Westerheijden 1990a).

The universities enrolled more than 352,000 full-time students and nearly 52,000 part-time students at the outset of the decade (Association of Commonwealth 1993). In recent years, institutions in Great Britain experienced rapid growth in student enrollments similar to that of the United States during the 1960s. Full-time enrollments also are increasing steadily, with an 11 percent gain between 1988–89 and 1990–91. Government projections of enrollment call for a 33 percent increase in demand by 2000 (Kells 1993).

Unlike their counterparts in the United States, British institutions tend to be quite small, averaging, as late as 1988, around 6,000 students (Johnes and Taylor 1990). At the outset of the decade, provisional expenditures for further and higher education in the U.K. reached £6.8 billion ($11 billion) (*Whitaker's Almanac* 1994).

Environmental context. Great Britain's higher education system of universities and public institutions has experienced a revolution of rising expectations during the past few decades. The introduction of performance indicators to the lexicon of higher education management in Great Britain marked a major shift in power that welcomed a conservative ideology to government in 1979. Government's perspective on higher education became one of "value for money," emphasizing economy, efficiency, and effectiveness (Goedegebuure, Maassen, and Westerheijden 1990a).

With rising inflation and a sluggish economy in the 1970s, the British government no longer could tolerate its system of block grant funding by the University Grants Committee (UGC). Cuts in government support in the early 1980s signaled a major shift in the way universities and colleges would be funded (Williams 1990), and the dramatic reduction in government funding and the elimination of block grants were strongly criticized within the academy (Kogan and Kogan 1983). A second major factor in the evolution of performance indicators was the publication of a government "green paper" ("Development of" 1985) that spoke to the use of indicators in the allocation of resources (Ball and Wilkinson 1992).

Suggestions for major organizational changes to higher education in a government "white paper," *Higher Education: A New Framework* (Dept. of Education and Science 1991), were incorporated in the Further and Higher Education Act of 1992 and the Further and Higher Education (Scotland) Act of 1992. These acts eliminated the binary system of higher education by removing the distinction between services provided by universities (funded in England and Wales through the Universities Funding Council) and by polytechnics and colleges (funded through the Polytechnics and Colleges Funding Council). All institutions in England, Scotland, and Wales are now funded through three Higher Education Funding Councils, which were empowered to obtain extensive institutional data in support of their allocation of funds (Green 1994, p. 4).

The new funding approach is sensitive to institutional missions. The former polytechnics, historically vocational in orientation, were to be judged against teaching performance as well as success in applied research. The older universities were expected to be assessed using a "research assessment exercise" that produces quality ratings of the universities' success in research (Universities Funding 1992). A fivefold rating scale of productivity in research was initiated in 1993 (Kells 1993), with criteria emphasizing international reputation as the key to the highest ratings. The methodology the councils use in funding research is based on quality of the research, the contract, and development. The research assessment exercise in 1992 produced a four-volume set of measures for use

The new funding approach is sensitive to institutional missions.

by the councils (Jongbloed and Westerheijden 1994).

The relationship between higher education and government continues to change, with a loosening of ties between institutions and local government (Brennan 1990). Despite these changes, the fear persists that the development of national indicators will inevitably "nationalize institutional policy making" (Ball and Wilkinson 1992, p. 11). The Further and Higher Education Act of 1992 fuels some of these fears. The capacity to gather and analyze data, for example, was greatly improved with the creation of a new central agency, the Higher Education Statistics Agency (HESA), which is charged with data collection in support of decisions by the funding councils.

Use of performance indicators. The British model blends external indicators with peer judgment to maintain quality assurance in higher education. Distinctions are drawn among quality audit, quality control, and quality assessment; responsibility for control rests with institutions, for audits with the Higher Education Quality Council, and for assessment with the new funding councils (Gordon 1992). Thus, a dual system of control exists: one administrative and the other professional (De Jager 1992).

In the past 25 years, normative mechanisms (a "clan" form of control by the academy) have been used as means of organizational control (Dill 1992; Ouchi 1989). The introduction of centralized indicators places additional pressure on institutional autonomy (Frackmann 1987; Kogan and Kogan 1983). Some critics argue that, for the former polytechnics, performance indicators represent the loss of academic control and the expansion of managerial control (McElwee 1992).

An important force influencing the allocation of resources for higher education in Great Britain was the concept of "competitive tendering" as a funding mechanism (McVicar 1990). In this approach, the state no longer was to provide a service; instead, it purchases student places that are subject to bid by service providers. England, Scotland, and Wales each appointed representatives to a funding council that acts as a purchasing agent of services based upon a complex allocation formula (Higher Education Funding 1993; Temple and Whitechurch 1994). Some argue, however, that increased reliance on student fees has eroded the power of the funding councils (McVicar 1990). Each university in Great Britain appears to be becoming more entrepreneurial as market forces of supply and demand replace national planning (Temple and Whitechurch 1994).

Multiple meanings and foci dot the landscape of performance indicators in Great Britain. The Committee of Vice Chancellors and Principals (CVCP) suggested three categories of quantitative measures: internal, external, and operational (Ball and Wilkinson 1992; Committee 1986). Each measure holds multiple meanings that often fail to provide "background information needed to interpret the data" (Harris and Dochy 1990).

Political culture and context appear to shape the focus of indicators (Sizer 1992), and the process of introducing performance indicators influenced the substance of the indicators themselves. They are neither value neutral nor process independent (Findlay 1990; Goedegebuure, Maassen, and Westerheijden 1990a). Critics have argued that most indicators reflect the ease of gathering data more than a conceptual framework (de Weert 1990; Elton 1987), rather than being developed through identifying the purposes to be served by the indicators, which in turn would shape the broader conceptual framework (Yorke 1991b).

The attitudes, beliefs, and values of key stakeholders concerning the role of education in society and the relationship between government and the educational community should determine the design of indicators. "The more the objectives behind higher education policy can be regarded as an expression of the more general political culture of a country, the more the policy—including any objectives [that] are part of it—will be accepted" (Sizer, Spee, and Bormans 1992, pp. 138–39). In the British public sector, government inspectors, rather than peers, are used to judge quality (Goedegebuure, Maassen, and Westerheijden 1990a). Gradually, the role of higher education has come to be viewed as an agent or force that should contribute to the national economy (Johnes and Taylor 1990).

Most indicators in the British initiative are expressions of a mechanistic view of education (Elton 1988). As a result, most can be grouped into measures of input, process, and output (Findlay 1990; Johnes and Taylor 1990). By 1992, the number of indicators had expanded to 65; although much of their emphasis is on input and proxy measures of process, measures of outcome, such as graduation and completion rates, are related directly to unit costs. Thus, cost per student is a common criterion consistent with the CVCP's management statistics model of performance indicators. The use of regression residuals provides a more sophisticated statistical approach to determine expected costs per student compared with actual costs (Johnes and Taylor 1990). Explanatory variables include "subject mix" to help explain variations in non-completion rates, institutional factors (faculty/student ratios and length of course study, for example), and the like. Similar to efforts in the United States, the systematic and comparative use of indicators should account for variations in students' abilities and the environmental context. Most critics argue that indicators should, but seldom do, flow from institutional mission (Cuenin 1987; Dochy and Segers 1990; Findlay 1990; Segers, Wijnen, and Dochy 1990), but while tailoring indicators to institutional mission is important, designers of indicator systems must be careful to minimize the development of performance indicators as "reductionist mechanisms" (Kells 1992a).

In the United Kingdom, performance indicators in general use include:

1. Number of applications per undergraduate place
2. Undergraduates' entry scores
3. Classification of or number of honors degrees awarded
4. Wastage rates of students
5. Staff workload
6. Employability of graduates
7. Postgraduate completion rates
8. Research grants and contracts
9. Research studentships awarded by prominent bodies, such as research councils
10. Records of publications
11. Students' loads
12. Staff/student ratios
13. Unit costs
14. Staff size by type
15. Institutional revenues and expenditures
16. Departmental equipment and recurrent grants and expenditures (Cuenin 1987; Kells 1990).

While the major focus has been on input variables, some effort is under way to assess productivity in research. Much of the work still uses traditional measures, such as peer reviews, publications, citation indices, and research revenues. Variations in research output are explained in part by process factors, such as ratios of research staff to total staff. Overall, much of the work uses process variables as explanatory variables in a classic regression equation of indicators. This approach appears to do little to examine systematically the direct link between inputs and outcomes, as the vast majority of the applications of performance indicators, whether focused on student outcomes or research output, develop proxy measures of process or conversion factors (Johnes and Taylor 1990; Kells 1990). Some success has been reported in developing process measures through periodic assessment of learning environments (Scottish Higher Education 1992).

Based on the input-process-output taxonomy, most indicators are highly quantitative and lend themselves easily to statistical manipulation, such as discriminate analysis of cost measures (De Jager 1992; Johnes and Taylor 1990). A lack of satisfactory cost allocation procedures to deal with the measurement of either effectiveness or efficiency remains, however (Cave, Kogan, and Hanney 1990). Because of limitations on the data's stability, inconsistent operationalization, and weak relationships to articulated goals, indicators are viewed as part of the machinery of "management technology" (Segers, Wijnen, and Dochy 1990).

A host of decision makers and policy makers currently consume data about performance indicators in Great Britain. Since 1984, the government has been particularly interested in improving the accountability of higher education in the eyes of taxpayers (Johnes and Taylor 1990). The net effect of the emphasis was an increased demand for information from institutions for use in allocation of resources. Not only do government decision makers use the data, however, as statistics about and performance indicators of university management have also found interest among consumers. The British use these quantifiable data in a table that compares institutions (Scottish Centrally Funded 1992). As a condition of developing or using such national data bases, information requirements of different management levels must be assessed and access negotiated (Sizer 1992).

While those in British higher education were familiar with reporting some type of performance data, much of the information was used historically more for administrative purposes than for management (Committee 1985; Spee and Bormans 1992). The Jarratt Committee's recommendation laid the groundwork for a shift in assumptions about governance of the academy and the resulting expansion of uses for performance data (Cave, Kogan, and Hanney 1990). Data were used originally as management statistics for descriptive purposes and later to allocate resources. In addition to the classic application of allocating resources, some have argued that the comparative assessment of institutions must not be a casual decision (Ball and Wilkinson 1992). When designed for use in allocation, multiple measures are preferred (Cave, Hanney, and Kogan 1991). The relationship between performance indicators and peer reviews should be complementary, with the former informing the latter (Sizer 1990b).

Observers have begun to note that the steady drift toward a bureaucratic model of higher education in Great Britain does little to benefit students if pedagogy is ignored (Barnett 1989; McElwee 1992). Whether interest in students' learning will increase, even if pedagogy is not ignored, remains uncertain (Muffo 1993). The Committee of Inquiry on Teaching Quality under the Polytechnics and Colleges Funding Council could be one signal of a renewed interest in the learning environment (Sizer 1990b). Other recent efforts are under way to introduce external assessment of program quality through work sponsored by the Funding Council in England, Scotland, and Wales. In addition, a system of quality audits is also under way through the Higher Education Quality Council (Yorke 1993), and similar interest has been demonstrated by the Council for National Academic Awards (Yorke 1991a). The Quality Audit group, formerly known as the Academic Audit Unit, is another approach to developing quality assessment within the institution. Reporting to the CVCP, its role is to review methods for monitoring and promoting academic standards among universities (Young 1990).

In 1992, macro performance indicators were developed for use with the former polytechnic schools. Four sets of performance indicators were developed in the areas of effectiveness, resources, efficiency, and source of funds (Kells 1993; Polytechnics 1992). The Universities Funding Council initiated a direct link between specialist panels and the use of indicators. This approach represents a clear, complementary relationship between quality assessment through peer judgment and external indicators. Further development of performance indicators will be coordinated through the recently established Joint Performance Indicators Working Group, whose initial focus of interest is teaching quality, use of space, financial health, research, and availability of data (Kells 1993).

Great Britain has begun to redefine the role of higher education, and as it moves from an elitist to a mass system of higher education, governments are likely to demand more information to measure value. The academy now finds itself competing for resources not only from government, but also from a marketplace filled with skeptical consumers.

Canada

Background. Covering nearly 3.9 million square miles with a population of more than 27.2 million by 1991, Canada in 1991–92 served a total of 554,021 students through 69 degree-granting institutions and 336,480 students through 203 publicly funded non-degree-granting institutions (*Europa* 1993). Enrollment in higher education increased steadily from 1982 through 1994 (Association of Commonwealth 1993). Support for higher education is provided mainly through the provinces, but because the provinces vary substantially in population, wealth, and, as a consequence, differential power, support for higher education has created an opportunity for the federal government to play an active role through the allocation of resources. The poor economic climate in Canada has created lower estimates of revenue, increased nondiscretionary expenditures, and reduced payments to the provinces. Tighter budgets created a climate of concern about requirements for resources in Canadian educational institutions (Association of Universities 1993), and subsequent funding for "equalization" has created the concomitant call for accountability (Association of Commonwealth 1993). Funding by the provinces accounts for about 69 percent of university expenditures, while the federal government contributes another 13.5 percent and student fees account for 10.2 percent.

Environmental context. The subject of quality assurance in general and the development of performance indicators in particular are best understood at the provincial and federal government levels. At the provincial level, performance indicators focus largely on issues of management; at the national level, the dominant project is the development of descriptive statistics in a program known as the Canada effort, supported by Statistics Canada/Council of Minister of Education (Canadian 1992; Kells 1992b).

Performance indicators have been developed in the context of the federal government's role in equalization, the regionalism of concentrated educational services, and the continuing issues of bilingualism and multiculturalism. Neither the universities nor the colleges form an integrated "system" of higher education, and universities in particular enjoy considerable autonomy in Canada.

Use of performance indicators. A key emerging policy issue involves maintaining access while controlling educational costs. Attempts to balance these two forces will find financial aid policies at one end of the continuum and the government's policies on the allocation of resources at the other. Some institutions plan to substantially increase tuition and fees as a way to recover shrinking support from provincial and federal governments. According to the Ontario Task Force on Accountability:

> *At one end of the spectrum is what might be termed "strict" accountability, when, for example, universities are held accountable by government for their expenditure of public funds by means of explicit rules and regulations. At the other end, there is what might more accurately be called "responsiveness," when, for example, universities are said to be accountable to their local community for providing social and cultural leadership* (Association of Universities 1993, p. 4).

In the early 1980s, provincial governments began to investigate the role of universities in their regions. The Bovey Commission, for example, sought to understand the role of universities in Ontario and their future plans. University responses laid the foundation for the development of performance indicators that, in turn, were helpful in comparative analyses and fundraising (Snowdon 1993).

Although federal and provincial governments continue the drive to install indicators, the media serve as an additional force. *Maclean's* magazine ranked 46 universities in a report that has further politicized the atmosphere (1992). As in the United States and western Europe, Canadian performance indicator systems reflect the existence of an enormous vacuum in the marketplace of higher education. Government officials and consumers demand better information about educational services, which can be provided by performance indicator systems (Snowdon 1993).

As economic pressures mount and student enrollments continue to increase, institutional and system performance indicators will shift from a focus on inputs to one on outcomes and their role in monitoring accountability and system performance (Association of Universities 1993). At least five approaches to quality currently dominate the field—political economy, productivity, value added, producer/consumer, content—with some eclectic approaches as well (Nadeau 1992). Indicators of quality and excellence can be defined as "those characteristics of all components of colleges and universities for which there is some consensus as to their contributions to the successful attainment of specific institutional missions and objectives" (p. 2).

The bulk of data collection nationally occurs in the federal government's Statistics Canada project. All performance indicator programs rely on the Statistics Canada data base for core information (Hawkins 1990), which includes data about students, academic staff, and finances. Data about students include standard demographic characteristics and degrees granted. Faculty records include data on demographics, degrees held, compensation, and principal subjects taught. Financial data include standard total expenditure profiles by fund and by type of expenditure and by function. While these three sets of files rely on the individual as the unit of observation, each college data base aggregates the individual files into institutional summaries.

Provinces have developed planning indicators to complement federal work. Among the provinces, Alberta's indicators emphasize institutional efficiency and effectiveness; British Columbia uses traditional indicators to measure accountability, assess program quality, and gauge efficiency; Newfoundland's measures compare systems, manage postsecondary education, and assess equity, effectiveness, and efficiency; and Ontario is developing indicators in the context of enhanced planning (Hawkins 1990). Provincial indicators will emphasize public objectives, while federal ones will focus primarily on monitoring education using descriptive measures (Hawkins 1990). While the need exists to incorporate mission-specific issues in the development of indicators, relatively little progress has been made. A partial explanation for the dependence on national management statistics is the sheer volume of data collected over the years; these national data sets may have distracted academic policy makers from more serious investigations of indicators.

A major impediment to the use of performance indicators in Canada is the difficulty in building a defensible rationale for comparing institutions, although interinstitutional and interprovincial comparisons are beginning to be implemented. Much of the literature about Canadian projects underscores the need for taking context into account and developing a classification of institutions as a basis for constructing indicators. In addition, the development of interprovincial comparisons remains suspect because integrity of the data remains suspect. Queen's University, however, developed an approach to ranking and comparisons with similar institutions, basing similarities on enrollment in undergraduate and graduate programs and the amount of sponsored research (Smith 1992). The success of the use of indicators at Queen's University might have been a function of senior management's quantitative orientation and the principal's interest in developing indicators (Snowdon 1993). Universitywide indicators, however, might not necessarily provide sufficient data to use in allocating resources (Nadeau 1992).

The design of indicator systems in Canada is similar to that in other developed nations, emphasizing primarily measures of either input or outcome. What little attention is paid to process factors is limited to traditional proxy ratio measures of conversion, such as student flow and length of studies. Equally significant, the measurement of process variables, defined by the learning environment, has not been systematic. A recent highly critical report of teaching, for example, encouraged uniform standards for evaluating teaching (Conference 1991; Smith 1991).

Australia
Background. Australian higher education consists of a unified system including some 40 institutions. Unlike institutions in the United States, all universities are secular in origin and established through action by the federal government (Asso-

ciation of Commonwealth 1993). The Australian Catholic University, although related to the church, is publicly funded and a member of the unified system. Australia also has a few private institutions and a handful of specialist institutions.

Total enrollment in higher education increased substantially in recent years, rising from 336,702 in 1981 to 534,538 a decade later. In addition, distance learning grew to 56,922 students in 1991. Employment opportunities, however, do not show the same pattern of growth, and unemployment countrywide was estimated at 11.2 percent in late 1992.

In 1992, the federal government allocated total funds of $A3.9 billion ($2.9 billion) to the universities. Funding occurs triennially on a rolling basis, with grants allocated as a single block (Association of Commonwealth 1993). The commonwealth's support for research increased to $A2.6 billion ($1.9 billion) in 1991–92.

Environmental context. The growing concern about quality in higher education in Europe appears to apply as well in Australia (Harman 1994; van Vught and Westerheijden 1992). Beginning with the federal government's decision in 1987 to develop a unified national system, Australian higher education is changing dramatically (Goedegebuure and Meek 1989). The country's emerging sense of the need to broaden its economic base through a stronger emphasis on international competitiveness brought higher education into sharp focus. Although the federal government did not have specific powers over education, its financial support has set the direction for higher education policy (Harman 1994). Intended to make higher education more responsive to the nation's economic development, the changes abolished the binary system, consolidated institutions, increased emphasis on applied sciences, targeted research, altered structures of governance, and promoted new ways to cut costs and develop alternative revenue streams. The primary instruments used to restructure higher education are financial incentives to reduce the number of institutions through mergers.

Australian institutions in the 1980s depended on government resources to a great extent, which served as an incentive to merge with other institutions to meet minimum enrollment standards. At the same time, the federal government sought to move from a highly regulated and centralized bureaucratic system to greater self-regulation, and a major change was the

Unlike in Great Britain, the Australian government's decision makers do not have a strong commitment to the philosophy of a free market.

introduction of a unified national system. The government's *Higher Education: A Policy Statement* (1988) called for greater flexibility among institutions in programs and areas of research, as well as more control over resources and some reallocation of funds based on performance in priority areas. In sum, "institutional autonomy and flexibility [were] juxtaposed with marketplace discipline" (Goedegebuure and Meek 1989, p. 221). Unlike in Great Britain, the Australian government's decision makers do not have a strong commitment to the philosophy of a free market (Teather 1990a).

Use of performance indicators. Although considerable scholarship has addressed the relationship of performance to quality assurance (Anwyl 1992; Burke 1993a), the government's initiatives have been conventional. Performance indicators are classified into three types: (1) internal indicators that focus on immediate postprogram performance (graduation rates), (2) operating indicators (class size), and (3) external indicators that focus on students' status after graduation (employment) (Commonwealth Tertiary Education 1989).

Like in Canada, performance indicators are not limited to information about students. Comparisons of research among universities include such measures as the number of journal publications, grants, books published, editorships, and citations (Grigg and Sheehan 1989), and the Performance Indicators Research Group was commissioned to develop an initial list of indicators to measure efficiency and effectiveness (Lindsay 1993). These initial and subsequent discussions focused on the development of information about performance as related to quality.

An initial set of 23 indicators was divided into three groups: (1) institutional context, such as characteristics of the academic staff, demand from students, their background, and cost data; (2) performance indicators, such as amount of teaching and learning, and research and professional service; and (3) indicators of social equity, such as gender ratios for staff and students (Lindsay 1993). A 1988 report of the Working Party recommends a series of indicators to measure institutional context and enhance the comparability of the findings across a range of institutions (Australian 1988).

Most of the measures are conventional operationalizations of input characteristics or outcomes. Some of the input variables can be conceptualized as measures of administrative process, such as ratios calculated on the relationship of numbers of acceptances to actual enrollments (sometimes called a yield ratio in the United States). Other input variables can be viewed as intermediate outcomes. For example, second-year retention and major sequence retention are components of student demand (Kells 1990).

Traditional measures of outcome track undergraduate and postgraduate performance, such as proportion of completions and the number of completions within two years. Measures of "destination outcomes" focus on employment status, postgraduate study, type of work, and salary. No data are collected to assess employers' perceptions of students' skills and competencies.

Only one measure addresses teaching quality, which is a perceptual item based on a limited set of performance characteristics. As with most systems, the difficult issue of weighting performance indicators remains unresolved. While the initial report of the Working Party called for experts to develop weights, others have argued for public disclosure of a methodology that could include statistical regression weighting (Hattie 1990). In addition, some concern has been expressed about the disciplinary bias toward the sciences that could occur as a result of research production indicators (Moses 1990).

Discipline reviews were introduced in the mid-1980s using senior academics, experts in various disciplines, and major employers of graduates. The initial experience with these reviews has been mixed, and some view the review process as very costly and time-consuming (Harman 1994; Higher Education Council 1992). A national academic audit mechanism is under development that is based on disciplinary panels rather than external examiners.

The quality assurance mechanism developed in Australia reflects a sensitivity to institutional autonomy. A quality assurance plan developed by the Committee for Quality Assurance in Higher Education (CQAHE) began with a study of quality assurance policies and practices. In 1994, the attention focused on teaching and learning. The quality review program is a serious commitment to funding quality programs. In 1994, for example, the program allocated $A76 million ($55.9 million) to those institutions that could "demonstrate effective quality assurance policies and practices and excellent outcomes" (O'Neil 1994). Efforts in 1995 should emphasize management as well as the integration of research and service. The CQAHE intends to assess outcomes at three levels: those associated with institutional missions, others related to the Higher Education Council's goal statements, and those reflecting the attributes of graduates and the impact of research (Lindsay 1994).

The relationship between performance indicators and quality remains underdeveloped. When quality is conceptualized as the measurement of the "worth" of something, the tendency is to limit the relationship to measures of outcome. This narrow view disregards other complementary avenues of connecting indicators to quality through reputation or content (Lindsay 1992, 1993). The Higher Education Council in Australia has raised the possibility of a national structure for quality assurance, and the National Board of Employment, Education, and Training published a paper in 1992 that lays the groundwork for an academic audit system that resembles work already under way in Great Britain (Gordon 1992; Higher Education Council 1992).

Some interest has been expressed in revisiting indicators to focus on "improving educational processes by attention to the many factors that influence student learning" (Lindsay 1993, p. 34; see also Higher Education Council 1992). The National Union of Students and the Council of Australian Postgraduate Associations endorsed the need for a broader perspective of measures.

The quality of the performance indicators developed to date has met with some criticism, including the underlying assumption of a single dimension to the measures (Hattie 1990) and some argument that the existing indicators are not sufficiently substantive in their relationship to higher education's goals, processes, and outcomes (Lindsay 1993). Others have expressed concern about the use of performance indicators to introduce systematic formula funding (Australian 1988; Hattie 1990). Subsequently, a higher education performance indicators research group was charged with defining performance indicators operationally (Cave, Hanney, and Kogan 1991), with performance indicators recommended by the group to be applied systemwide (Linke 1990). Another continuing problem is the lack of a defensible approach to building valid comparison groups (Linke 1990).

Developments in Australia mirror concerns expressed in other countries in applying a mechanistic view of higher education that produces measures of input, process, and outcome. Concern has been expressed about the weakness of process measures, especially in the context of the complexity of higher education (Linke 1992).

Few efforts are under way to address the difficult area of process measurement. One recent work refers to procedural characteristics that might form baseline principles of good practice in some expression of formative evaluation, and offers a checklist of procedures that constitute good practice in process (Hattie 1990). The notion of process can be viewed from the perspective of managerial performance or characteristics of the learning environment. Whether procedural differences explain variations in student performance outcomes remains an unaddressed empirical question. Some have questioned whether process measures should be used directly as performance indicators (Cullen 1987).

A major problem facing the development of performance indicators in Australia is the availability of reliable data for comparative analysis (Doyle 1994; Kells 1993). A recently released major report has been developed on a set of equity indicators that augment the set of general performance indicators (Martin 1994). The report is the product of a project funded by the Department of Employment, Education, and Training to provide operational definitions for a wide range of performance indicators across functional areas within institutions of higher education and should provide considerable support for improved institutional management information systems.

The swift movement to a unified system, the number of mergers, and related policy changes have altered the landscape of higher education in Australia. It remains uncertain whether these changes will result in less diversity in programs and an increased reliance on quantitative indicators of systematic, institutional, or departmental quality. The Working Party on Performance Indicators suggests that "to reduce funds as a penalty for poor performance would make the graduates cheaper but almost certainly worse" (Teather 1990b, p. 119). At this stage of performance indicators' development in Australia, the basic indicators will reflect stakeholders' perceptions of the uses and purposes to be served by the system, the financial dependency of institutions, and the political ideology of government decision makers. One can only speculate on whether the government can transform higher education into an economic and social engine for systematic change. Recent funding patterns suggest that government decision makers will maintain a strong hand while allowing some participation in the definition of the journey.

The Netherlands
Background. Dutch higher education has two distinct segments (Bormans et al. 1990). Universities prepare students for independent scientific careers in an academic or professional setting, while HBO (*hoger beroeps onderwigs*) institutes emphasize training in applied science for specific occupations. Currently, 20 universities, including seven theological institutions, and 87 HBO institutes serve the Netherlands (Kells 1992b). The Open University was developed to provide university degrees, HBO programs, and other courses, mainly through distance education. Government funding of higher education accounts for approximately 90 percent of an institution's total budget (Westerheijden 1990). Core institutional budgets are allocated as a lump sum and used freely, while capital budgets are strictly earmarked (Frederiks, Westerheijden, and Weusthof 1994).

Environmental context. Since the early 1980s, the Dutch government has developed a number of major policy proposals designed to restructure its strategy toward higher education. A number of reasons are behind the new strategy, including the ideological preferences of the political coalition in power since 1982 and the problematic budgetary situation facing the government (Maassen and van Vught 1988). While these circumstances are similar to those of other social democratic countries like Sweden and Denmark, the Dutch response is unusual, because it directly links expanded institutional autonomy with more stringent standards of quality (Sander 1993). One of the main shifts in government policy toward higher education is an increasing demand for greater relevance to society (Bormans et al. 1990). The government wishes to encourage universities to supply needed workers for science and industry while generating new knowledge and technology to benefit the economy.

The Secretary of Education and Sciences issued a report on higher education, autonomy, and quality in 1985 to emphasize quality in research and instruction through increased accountability (Drenth, Van Os, and Bernaert 1989).

The report called for a new approach to managing higher education for a number of reasons:

1. Government regulations were leading to inflexible, cumbersome procedures;
2. Institutional responsibilities were too restricted; and
3. Quality measurement and assurance were inadequate (Dochy, Segers, and Wijnen 1990b).

In 1988, the Ministry of Education and Science translated this broad government policy into the Higher Education and Research Act, which contains the following components:

1. Greater institutional autonomy in the design and implementation of new curricula to encourage innovation and diversity;
2. A system of quality assessment leading to public information on the quality of teaching and research at each institution to enhance competition;
3. A strengthened system of open access to all graduates of higher forms of secondary education;
4. Possible government response to an imbalance in the supply of students and the demand for courses offered and positions in the labor market by centrally reducing the number of students in a discipline;
5. Maintenance of the government's role as principal funder of public higher education (Bormans et al. 1990).

The system is administered by the Association of Cooperating Universities (the *Vereniging van Samenwerkende Nederlandse Universiteiten*), a quasi-public higher education association, as a formative evaluation of study programs every six years (Jongbloed and Westerheijden 1994). In 1993, the Higher Education and Research Act was codified into law, formally reducing government control over operational details while maintaining final responsibility for major issues of funding and length of program (Goedegebuure et al. 1993).

Use of performance indicators. The system of quality assessment was tested in 1988 in four disciplines (Westerheijden 1990). The process consisted of three major stages:

1. Self-evaluation by faculties;
2. Comparison among faculties by visiting review committees;
3. Institutional response to the committee's findings.

In addition to self-study reports by the institutions, the Association of Cooperating Universities added a "fact book" of centralized data that includes several performance indicators. Through the Higher Education and Research Plan, the government intended to design performance indicators as operational instruments for:

1. Evaluation to show the extent the government's goals have been achieved;
2. Monitoring of relevant developments and trends;
3. Dialogue of objective information;
4. Funding (Cave, Hanney, and Kogan 1991).

The fact books were not well received, because they contained incomplete data, discrepancies with institutional data, and ambiguous interpretations of data (Westerheijden 1990). Consequently, the association established a steering committee to examine indicators and propose their future use in a new quality control system (Kells 1992b). Researchers, however, continue to disagree on the use of performance indicators in quality assurance and debate their operational validity.

Others support a system of quality assessment based on peer review rather than performance indicators (Vroeijenstijn and Acherman 1990), suggesting the examination of the fundamental goals driving quality assessment and reliance on assessment tools consistent with those objectives. While performance indicators might be perceived as helpful in measuring outcomes of governmental policies (with an orientation toward control), peer review provides the best advice for the enhancement of institutions (an orientation toward improvement) (Vroeijenstijn and Acherman 1990). Additional criticism of indicators includes the lack of connection between indicators and actual performance and the fear that indicators ultimately become standards for performance.

Others also call for a strengthened system of peer review but assert that increased assessment requires objective information (Paardekooper and Spee 1990). They do not consider peer review and performance indicators incompatible elements in assessment but believe that judgments of quality by experts can carry greater authority if they are based on knowledge of the facts. If assessments are to determine the future capacity of institutions in addition to the usual review of past performance, then it will be even more essential to include a sound empirical perspective with the assessment made by academic peers.

The most comprehensive debate surrounding development of the assessment plan has centered on the introduction of performance indicators (Cave, Hanney, and Kogan 1991). Implementation has been difficult because of widespread skepticism about the validity and utility of indicators and because of an absence of existing indicators for education in general rather than the predominance of performance indicators for research. A tentative list of 26 indicators was published in 1988 with a ranking order of the universities for each, but the list was criticized because changes over time were reflected only in each institution's relative position compared to others (penalizing universities that performed well initially) and because it was unclear what some indicators were intended to measure. While the government might be pushing the use of performance indicators to achieve its higher education goals, the main policy thrust remains the establishment of systematic self-assessment and external review (Cave, Hanney, and Kogan 1991).

The publication of these initial indicators led to many suggestions for further improvement and development of performance indicators:

1. The purposes of indicators should be explicit.
2. Indicators based on changes should not reflect badly on institutions with good early performance.
3. Rankings based on specific indicators should be avoided.
4. Use of indicators to diminish necessary discussion within and among institutions should also be avoided (Bormans et al. 1990).

Further refinement of performance indicators will permit the government's withdrawal from management of processes, while gaining greater control of product management (Maassen and van Vught 1988). This shift in government planning and control will result in a more output-oriented "mission funding" mechanism for Dutch higher education. The government is willing to encourage the formative nature of quality assessment by not penalizing negative results from self-evaluations or reports from peer groups (van Vught and Westerheijden 1993). Only repeated deficiencies over multiple review cycles would result in decreased funding.

Performance indicators currently are used very little in setting Dutch higher education policy through quality assessment (Jongbloed and Westerheijden 1994). Indicators do play a critical role in funding, however, in determining the amount of core funds to award universities and HBOs. Since January 1993, a new system has been employed for funding core teaching and research, with the following indicators directly determining a major portion of core funds appropriated to each institution:

- *Teaching indicators:* Number of registered students; length of study; number of degrees awarded
- *Research indicators:* Number of doctoral theses; number of certificates to design engineers.

Thus, performance indicators play a very minor role in shaping discussion and policy regarding quality assessment in the Netherlands, but a handful of indicators are critical in determining core funding for higher education.

Finland
Background. Finland has 20 university-level institutions with approximately 100,000 students (Niiniluoto 1990). Organized national policy and a strong belief in national planning have characterized the Finnish system of higher education since the 1960s. Developments within higher education over the past 20 years include regional expansion, democratization of university administration, mission-oriented research promoting social progress, and reform in curricula intended to narrow the gap between academic and vocational education. While each university has some degree of autonomy in its internal affairs, the Ministry of Education serves as the central unit of administration for higher education (Kells 1992b).

Environmental context. Like many European countries, the expansion of Finland's university system during the 1960s was partly motivated by expanding democratization (Stolte-

Heiskanen 1992). This growing trend put pressure on higher education to broaden access to wider segments of the population and to provide a more diversified and qualified workforce, particularly in scientific and technological fields. These new demands have resulted in a functional overload, where universities attempt too many things without changing the structure of the institution and are simultaneously faced with increasing demands for efficiency and accountability.

General planning for higher education is based on the Special Development Plan for Higher Education and the National Medium-Term Economic Plan (Niiniluoto 1990). The government approves the development plan every four years, establishing overall objectives for the development of higher education:

1. Areas of activity selected for emphasis;
2. Specific development projects in research and teaching; and
3. Changes in numbers of students.

Each university also has a medium-term plan that is coordinated with a general economic plan for higher education and the national medium-term plan (Hüfner and Rau 1987). The Higher Education Development Act of 1987 guaranteed an annual increase of 15 percent in funding for research and postgraduate studies during a five-year period—on the condition that a university's performance be accountable and evaluated. Resource planning, efficiency, flexibility, leadership, and accountability have become key descriptors of current higher education policy in Finland.

Use of performance indicators. The Higher Education Development Act of 1987 directed all higher education institutions to apply a system of performance evaluation resulting in sufficient and comparable data on outputs and costs of institutional activities (Cave, Hanney, and Kogan 1991). The Ministry of Education's working group on improving the methods of evaluating the performance of universities observed that a variety of data related to university productivity had been collected and stored by different authorities. The group identified a number of problems with the existing data collection process, including overlapping work, slow availability of information, difficulties in comparing data, and the lack of data use in planning (Niiniluoto 1990).

Organized national policy and a strong belief in national planning have characterized the Finnish system.

In response to the recommendations of the working group, the Ministry of Education created a data base to be used as a public clearinghouse for data about higher education. The information is reported by institution, with no departmental or individual data, and contains basic definitions. Available data from 1981 to the present include:

1. Number of students
2. Number of degrees conferred (masters, licentiate, doctorate)
3. Staff by rank
4. Costs
5. Supplementary training courses
6. Space and facilities (Kells 1992b).

Beginning in 1988, three data elements were added: sources of income other than budgeted funds, scientific publications, and research fellows working abroad. The working group proposed the creation of additional data bases at universities that would include certain information by department: number of teaching and research personnel, expenditures by department, research financed by outside sources, and scientific activities. While the scientific community is critical and suspicious of the use of performance indicators as a result of the lack of prior discussion concerning their use in evaluation (Niiniluoto 1990), the general sense is that indicators could prove to be useful tools if developed and applied to increase the high quality of teaching and research (Kells 1992a).

Although the evaluation system is still being refined in Finland, the principle of rewarding efficient institutions and departments has already begun (Cave, Hanney, and Kogan 1991). Institutions receive additional funding as a reward for their production of graduates who engage in research and postgraduate research training. State officials are generally content to leave the educational system alone and to effect change through marginal increments (Stolte-Heiskanen 1992). As such, the development of performance indicators in Finland has focused on aggregate measures without serious concern about institutional contexts and dynamics. Future attempts to develop indicators should focus on processes rather than inputs and outputs. The government's top-down approach to developing performance indicators (Höltta 1988) results in no understanding of the complexities in educational processes or the many dimensions of outcomes in the production of knowledge. The next few years will be critical for Finnish higher education as administrators attempt to find a balance between state and academic control.

Sweden

Background. Since reform in 1977, Swedish higher education has consisted of an integrated system that includes traditional university studies, former professional colleges, and a number of study programs previously offered by the secondary school system (Bauer 1990). Currently, Sweden has 31 institutions operated by the central government at 21 locations (Furumart 1989). The creation of a single comprehensive system of postsecondary education resulted from a need to reduce the differences in status between postsecondary sectors and to respond to requirements of rational planning (Kells 1992b). The National Board of Universities and Colleges serves as the central government authority for higher education and research. Approximately 184,000 students attend Swedish higher education institutions, an increase of 25,000 from 1990 to 1993 (Sander 1994a).

Environmental context. The National Board initiated a project to foster self-study and self-evaluation among departments and institutions (Cave, Hanney, and Kogan 1991). Workshops that provided simulation exercises in trimming budgets highlighted the difficulties in coping with conflicting goals and in establishing measures of quality while relating to harsh economic realities. This move to increased decentralization has resulted in greater autonomy for universities and university colleges, particularly through increased responsibility for planning, allocation of resources, and development (Sizer, Spee, and Bormans 1992). State budgeting systems are also being changed, resulting in more lump-sum funding to institutions.

This decentralization does not mean that the government plans to relinquish all control of postsecondary education (Bauer 1990). Indeed, the intended change is from management by instruction to management by objectives—which requires more systematic evaluation than has previously been present in Swedish higher education. Responsibility for follow-up, quality control, and audits of activity has also been given to individual institutions. Naturally, evaluation and methodologies have been high priorities for discussion, including the development and use of performance indicators.

Swedish scholars are questioning the uses of institutional self-evaluation (Furumart 1989). Some contend that evaluations should not provide information to government authorities for their decision making, nor should it be a process for institutional assessment of efficiency, quality, and performance to outside parties. They view self-evaluation as an internal affair designed to provide a sound basis for institutional decisions.

Use of performance indicators. Rather than building a completely new system of evaluation for higher education, authorities proposed that Sweden build on the better forms of evaluation already in existence (Bauer 1990). A fundamental component of this system would be the National Board's annual report on higher education, which synthesizes data submitted by all universities and colleges on the use of resources and its results. The statistical data that have been regularly collected and published in the annual report include:

1. Number of student equivalents provided
2. Number of student equivalents used
3. Number of annual student equivalents provided
4. Number of annual student equivalents used
5. Total credit production
6. Total expenditures
7. Total number of graduations (Kells 1992b).

Swedish policy, however, does not specify the kind of performance information to be provided by the institutions (Cave, Hanney, and Kogan 1991). Government legislation in 1988 called for the development of yardsticks to compare Swedish higher education and research to other countries. These measures, however, do not rank institutions and do not link quality control to processes within higher education.

National elections in September 1994 marked the return to political control by Social Democrats after a three-year shift to a center-right coalition and their move to decentralize Swedish higher education (Sander 1994a). The return of socialist leadership, however, will not eliminate the use of performance indicators and an emphasis on accountability. Rather, to allocate funds to institutions, the use of indicators like examination results and the number of students graduating will continue, while quantitative measures will be eliminated from assessments of quality.

Denmark

Background. Denmark has five traditional universities, as well as 12 other institutions offering university-level instruction (Sander 1994b). The higher education system enrolls approximately 156,000 students, or about 15 percent of the college-age population. University-level institutions can be public or private, with a Board of Governors overseeing the private institutions and a Rector appointed by the Ministry of Education governing the public institutions (Bache and Maassen 1993). Government funding accounts for 100 percent of teaching expenditures in higher education, with funding increasingly moving to a lump-sum allocation.

Environmental context. The University Administration Act of 1970 gave significant influence to students in the governance of universities. Critics called for stronger management of the higher education sector, which resulted in Parliament's giving the Minister of Education power in 1976 to regulate access and fix student numbers in broad program areas (Kells 1992b). This initiative by the ministry has improved control of the budget and helped balance higher education programs with the needs of the labor market. Nevertheless, the current system has a number of persistent weaknesses:

1. Teaching and research are budgeted separately, but the Ministry does not know how the appropriations are used. The Ministry uses budget figures only, not accounting figures.
2. No centrally fixed teaching load exists, and each collegiate body decides the amount of resources allocated for teaching.
3. Often the institutions themselves are not aware of the consequences of their elaborate systems to allocate teaching loads and resources. No accurate information exists on how teachers spend their working time.
4. Between 40 and 60 percent of professional resources are allocated to research, but little is known about research output and the quality of research.

5. The Ministry is responsible for most of the buildings, and it is not possible to assess general costs and compare them with similar information for other institutions.
6. The Ministry does not have easy access to information on mobility and age of personnel.
7. No comparable information exists on study programs among the various institutions (Von Linstow 1990).

In response to these concerns, the Ministry began to make the system more flexible and responsive to the needs of society, while calling for greater accountability from universities (Sizer 1992). In addition, the Ministry created a general computer-based information system to serve as a tool in the daily management of institutions and the overall management of higher education. While the words "performance indicators" were not used at that time, the Ministry wants to have this type of information (Kells 1993).

State funding of higher education has been streamlined, with half of each institutional budget automatically awarded each year and the rest tied to the production of graduates (Sander 1994b). This concern for the small annual number of graduating students was based on most students' slow pace of completion and on the frequent interruptions in their program of study.

Use of performance indicators. In 1990, the Danish government released a plan, "An Open Market for Higher Education," which emphasizes a supervisory role for government and a decentralized, market-driven system for universities and students (Bache and Maassen 1993). The 1990 plan was codified in a 1992 law requiring external evaluation of teaching quality in response to decentralization (Frederiks, Westerheijden, and Weusthof 1994). This exchange of assessment for autonomy differs from the Dutch system, however, as Danish universities did not respond to government initiatives. Consequently, a government-funded independent agency was created to coordinate the quality assessment system (Sander 1994b). The evaluation program is administered by independent educators and professionals in Denmark. A major feature of the assessment is the collection of data from students, graduates, and employers to determine "customer satisfaction" at a national level, but no direct feedback is given to institutions. To date, institutions have strongly rejected attempts to incorporate performance indicators into evaluations (Sizer 1992), and tensions will continue between the government and institutions as long as the indicators are meant both to give internal insight and to provide information for external decisions (Sizer, Spee, and Bormans 1992). The Ministry has taken charge of the performance indicator project to ensure satisfactory solutions to the problem. The Danish experience illustrates the need to collaborate and cooperate when developing useful data that all parties can use (Kells 1993).

A Comparison of International Indicator Systems

Table 8 summarizes the use of performance indicators in the seven countries discussed in this section. For each country, nine comparative criteria are applied (see also Nedwek and Neal 1994b). The criteria are not intended to assess the relative merits of each approach but to summarize trends based on available research literature.

This sample of initiatives mirrors a number of themes discussed earlier (Nedwek and Neal 1994b). First, indicators primarily are variations of measures of input and outcomes. This mechanistic view of data selection could be driven by most initiatives' emphasis on accountability and by the close connection between accountability and budgeting. Inputs and outcomes most closely resemble the emphasis on allocations of most appropriations processes.

Second, a remarkable similarity exists in the use of performance indicators, regardless of the geographical setting. Despite differences in the size, scale, and complexity of the state higher education system, the indicators and approaches to their use are very similar in format, focus, and dissemination. But there are other similarities:

1. Organizational control seems to be hierarchical during development of the model. Early indications from Great Britain suggest a movement to market control once the system matures.
2. The primary use of performance indicators focuses on monitoring existing systems.
3. The models are built on indirect connections to students' learning, or an assumed leap of faith that outcomes can be attributed to processes in the institution.

TABLE 8

NINE CRITERIA FOR PERFORMANCE INDICATORS
APPLIED TO SEVEN COUNTRIES

Criteria	Great Britain	Canada	Australia	Netherlands	Finland	Sweden	Denmark
1. *Locus of Control:* Clan, hierarchical, or market emphasis	Hierarchical with market emphasis	Hierarchical	Hierarchical	Clan and governmental hierarchical	Hierarchical	Hierarchical	Clan
2. *Degree of Governmental Control/Involvement:* Direct, indirect, laissez-faire	Direct	Direct	Direct	Indirect	Direct	Direct	Laissez-faire
3. *Focus of Performance Indicators:* Institutional effectiveness, efficiency, economy	Efficiency	Effectiveness and efficiency	Effectiveness and efficiency	Effectiveness	Efficiency	Efficiency	Effectiveness
4. *Sources of Variation in Quality:* Emphasis on special or common causes	Common	Common	Common	Common	Common	Common	Common
5. *Data Selection, Methods of Gathering Data, Levels of Aggregation:* Input, process, outcomes	Emphasizes input	Inputs and outcomes	Inputs and outcomes	Inputs and outcomes	Outcomes	Outcomes	Outcomes
6. *Intended Audience(s):* Internal or external decision makers and policy makers	External policy makers	Internal and external decision makers	Internal and external decision makers	External decision makers	External policy makers	External decision makers	External policy makers
7. *Emphasis of Use:* Monitoring, measuring progress, forecasting, diagnosing, allocating, manipulating symbols	Monitoring and allocating	Monitoring	Monitoring	Monitoring and forecasting	Monitoring and forecasting	Monitoring	Monitoring
8. *Intended Impact on Students' Learning:* Direct, indirect, assumed	Assumed	Assumed	Indirect	Indirect	Assumed	Assumed	Assumed
9. *Relationship to Institutional Mission:* Direct, indirect, or assumed link between mission and system design	Assumed	Assumed	Indirect	Direct	Indirect	Indirect	Direct

This overview of existing performance indicator systems helps clarify practices around the world. A study of five of the countries discussed in this section is the basis for the following ten suggestions to facilitate funding agencies' development and use of performance indicators in relationships between governments and institutions:

> *1. It is important for a government to spend time clearly specifying and communicating its objectives and policies for the higher education system [before] discussing with insti-*

tutions the development and use of a system of perfor-
mance indicators.

2. *Government should stimulate discussions with institutions*
to encourage identification of institutional objectives in
the context of government policies so as to identify areas
of agreement on criteria for assessing achievements.

3. *It is important for a government at an early stage to*
explain fully to institutions the uses . . . it intends to make
of performance indicators as part of the process of se-
curing institutional acceptance of their use for assessing
achievements.

4. *It is important to invest time and resources on developing*
jointly with institutional representatives a sound concep-
tual basis for subsequent development, including defining
the nature, purpose, and limitations of each indicator.

5. *To build a reliable data base, it is important to start from*
the needs for data within institutions . . . to secure an
interest and active participation in the development and
operation of the data base.

6. *. . . To lessen tensions that [could] arise in diverse and*
selective systems, it is a prerequisite to make a distinction
between the information requirements of different levels
of management (faculty, institution, and national) and
accept that not all management statistics in the national
data base should be available for use by national bodies.

7. *If the funding model is based on equality of opportunity,*
funding, and comparable quality of institutions and
courses, . . . the primary purposes of assistance to insti-
tutional managers and the provision of relevant and re-
liable data that [account] for regional and special insti-
tutional factors [should be emphasized].

8. *[Institutions should be involved] in the review of existing*
or the development of new resource allocation models.

9. *[It should be recognized] that comparable teaching quality*
assurance systems informed by agreed performance indi-
cators are best developed by the institutions if their owner-
ship is to be secured or ownership is vested in an inde-
pendent body.

10. It might be natural and necessary for government to start
the process of developing a national system of performance indicators but afterward leave it to the institutions
of higher education to develop proposals on how they
will fulfill the demands (Sizer 1992, pp. 156–63).

Summary

International state higher education systems are diverse in size, scope, and mission, while international applications of performance indicators conversely present numerous similarities in the context, development, and use of such accountability measures. Increased fiscal constraints, a call for relevancy to the workplace, and a growing concern for return on the public's investment have all shaped the development of performance indicator systems in the countries examined in this section. The final section builds on this international survey to probe future implications for policy and practice.

CHALLENGES FOR THE REST OF THE 1990s

Limited resources, rising expectations, and a growing awareness of the interconnectedness of educational systems have
implications for higher education and how its stakeholders
will respond to heightened calls for public accountability.
The cynic will dismiss or deny the moment, calling accountability and quality assurance yet one more fad foisted upon
underpaid faculty by a burgeoning bureaucracy. The hard-
pressed, sincere policy maker will wonder whether performance systems improve the quality of the learning environment enough to justify their increasing costs. Other less har-
dened or less cynical observers, inside and outside the
academy, might view the remaining half of the 1990s as a rare
and narrow window of opportunity to reinforce and revitalize
one of society's core functions—higher education.

Rankings based on reputation appear to have served more symbolic than informational expectations of management.

The academy is beginning to understand that "getting back
to basics" means far more than the three R's of elementary
and secondary education. It includes revitalizing a sense of
academic integrity and, albeit reluctantly, providing more
collective responsibility through a coherent, quality curriculum with an effective cadre of faculty. Expectations for authentic education, a revitalized faculty embracing new roles,
and more learning for fewer government dollars have trans-
formed the issues of the 1970s and 1980s from access to
concerns about and assessment of productivity, quality,
and accountability.

We need to remind ourselves that the academy, unlike policy makers and other stakeholders in the community, has
always seen fit—by one means or another—to gauge how
well it is doing. For most of this century, higher education
sought ways to determine quality and to compare performance among a set of institutions. The current interest in performance indicators, in a sense, represents another tool for
measuring and monitoring quality. But it appears that the purposes of performance indicators have changed over the past
half century. Rankings based on reputation appear to have
served more symbolic than informational expectations of
management. Rankings served as "brag sheets," providing
only a loose connection to performance (Dooris and Teeter
1994), and discussions of reputation served as unobtrusive
measures of influence within the academy.

Performance indicators were later used to improve decisions about the allocation of resources, especially through
use of tools developed by the National Center for Higher Edu-

---

cation Management Systems. More recently, indicators have been used to design strategies for containing costs (Turk 1992) and to increase efficiency in the use of resources (Rush 1992). These newer tools, however, represent a significant departure from earlier methodologies, especially techniques to measure reputation, as performance indicators have melded quality assurance with accountability to external stakeholders. Having moved beyond symbolism and indirect measures of influence, the newer tools have brought greater politicization, because the stakes are now much higher.

In addition to the link to accountability, performance indicators appear to provide a more serious appraisal of performance then the earlier methodologies. Even the more rigorous approaches undertaken by regional or professional accreditation bodies have not enjoyed consistent support as the preferred methodology for achieving quality assurance. The "clubbiness" of higher education (Ewell 1994a), a tradition of highly abbreviated site visits, and the potential for politicizing self-study teams in some regions of the United States remain a problem.

Short-term Future Trends

Given this brief look at the recent past and a sample of applications on three continents, what can higher education administrators expect in the future? Four recent trends will help shape the future of the academy, particularly in the United States, and discussions about quality assurance and accountability (Ewell 1994a). First, higher education will continue to be viewed as a key asset. Second, accountability in the K–12 arena will remain more specific and focused, while higher education will continue facing a crisis of confidence from policy makers. Third, the dominant focus will return to undergraduate education, especially the general education component of the curriculum and graduates' skills. Fourth, higher education will remain driven by the market and highly sensitive to community support.

This overview of quality assurance programs and performance indicator initiatives in North America, western Europe, and Australia suggests several other themes and trends. What then lies ahead? The remainder of this section explores some of these themes and their implications for the higher education community.

First, performance indicators could achieve influence beyond their preponderant use as symbols to satisfy discontented policy makers and consumers, becoming instead powerful tools that complement existing quality assurance practices. The explosion of indicators, opportunities for comparative assessments, and increased standardization of key indicators and their definitions suggest greater use of performance indicators in allocating resources.

Second, these new tools could be useful beyond meeting the information needs of governing boards and policy makers. It is reasonable to suggest that indicators could be useful for consumers of higher education. Better information in the hands of parents, counselors, and students remains in high demand. Similarly, industrial leaders as board members, philanthropic agencies with their emphasis on restricted giving, and bond underwriters see the potential for accessing better data on institutional performance.

Third, as patterns of usage continue to evolve, it appears that mandates for accountability are the primary focus, while improvement to academic processes remains somewhat secondary, largely because of difficulties with integrating such measures in the design of performance indicators. Total quality management and continuous process improvement held promise as potential proxies of assessing academic process, but they have failed for the most part to become part of management cultures in higher education. Applications are far more successful in classic business functional areas than in pedagogic settings (Dooris and Teeter 1994; Teeter and Lozier 1993).

The future seems to support continued reliance on administrative rather than professional accountability (Edgerton 1993a, 1993b). The use of "league tables" in Europe and North America (Webster 1992), for example, is creating an atmosphere of superimposed, external standards of excellence. Because so many systems of performance indicators serve to monitor and control operations, it is more likely that the second half of the 1990s will bring continued emphasis on bureaucratic accountability than on professional accountability. Current incentives provided to faculty do not encourage collective responsibility for quality in the academy. The faculty *will* use data from performance indicators but only when more incentives exist for doing so. The best potential for professional accountability might be through revisiting performance standards within the academy. Decisions about rank and tenure, for example, that are more sensitive to the heightened interest in excellent teaching of undergraduates could help restore more faith and trust in the academy for students and other consumers.

Fourth, given the fads that have marked higher education management circles—management by objective, zero-base budgeting, planning/programming/budgeting systems, for example—it remains highly unlikely that performance indicators in institutions will create enough broad-based support to sustain a reform movement. If performance indicators are integrated with broader requirements for information, however, it is possible that they can become more useful as management tools (Borden and Banta 1994).

As organizations and educational systems move toward a network approach to the functioning of organizations, managers will need to adjust accordingly. A networked organization will demand that managers:

1. Respond more rapidly to new situations, such as demographic changes;
2. Handle conflict and uncertainty where lines of authority and decision making are blurred;
3. Learn higher-order skills in analysis and conceptualization;
4. Learn how to work in problem-focused teams;
5. Use systems of measurement that are sensitive to cooperative working environments;
6. Share resources and nurture diffuse accountability;
7. Use information technology to move information to decision makers more rapidly and within narrower planning cycles; and
8. Obtain the technology infrastructure to support emerging data management systems (Rockart and Short 1990).

Performance indicator systems can serve as potentially useful *tools* in the emerging cooperative work environments.

Performance indicator systems can help create greater attention to context and mission, articulating rules for decision making in building comparison groups, making data more actionable, and developing a stronger conceptual and theoretical base. The issue will be whether managers can be developed rapidly enough to take advantage of the information. Were indicator systems to be used as quick solutions to complex problems, however (for example, acting as threshold standards for decisions about funding), policy makers and decision makers would quickly find themselves in a nonproductive, adversarial environment.

Fifth, the tension between further centralization or renewed interest in decentralization will remain strong. Greater centralization, particularly at the state level, accompanied by growth in the use of performance indicator systems appears more likely to continue in the United States, but a reversal of that approach could soon appear in Europe. Part H of the 1992 amendments to the U.S. Higher Education Act encourages the federal government to set standards in areas traditionally reserved to institutions, for example, defining students' satisfactory progress as taking 150 percent of the published time to complete a program. Schools must also demonstrate that less than a third of their undergraduates withdraw during the regular academic year. In addition, state regulatory language must include quantifiable standards for completion and graduation rates. Equally significant, accreditation officials are empowered to conduct unannounced site visits to all institutions with vocational programs.

Although the U.S. Department of Education retreated considerably from earlier drafts of the regulations for Part H, the greater federalization of higher education in the United States is likely to continue. While state postsecondary review entities are mandated to develop specific indicators to monitor higher education institutions at the state level, standards set by SPREs must be reviewed and approved by the federal government. And other federal legislation reinforces the theme of centralization. For example, the Student Right-to-Know and Campus Security Act requires reporting data about graduation rates and frequency of crimes' occurring. Policy makers' perceptions that higher education has not adequately reformed itself internally and that supporting agencies like accrediting bodies are not up to the task have encouraged this shift in the locus of control.

Several European developments, in contrast, suggest renewed interest in quality assurance models that involve members of the academy. Quality audits by peers, somewhat akin to visits by accreditation teams in the United States, remain a viable way for an institution to assess performance. It is difficult to speculate whether external performance indicator systems can be used to complement the work of such auditing teams. It might well be that different types of institutions will be encouraged to develop institutional indicators or to select measures from existing national indicator systems that fit their distinct mission. The demand for increased quality while offering increased autonomy in countries such as the Netherlands certainly provides attractive alternatives. With the exception of a few outcome measures associated with core funding decisions, performance indicators are little used by the Dutch. More important, the number of indicators is kept relatively small, reflecting the government's view that its involvement in the affairs of higher education should be kept to a minimum (Jongbloed and Westerheijden 1994).

Sixth, access to administrative performance systems through networks within and among continents will accelerate in the last half of the 1990s. Developments in hardware and software can now support access to high-volume transaction processing and the creation of mammoth frozen files. Historically disparate data bases are becoming accessible through new languages. These rapid technological changes will increase the potential for use of systemic performance indicators across a range of core institutional functions and locations.

Seventh, awareness is growing about the seamlessness of all education—K–12 through postsecondary—and across political borders, but it is unclear whether future indicator systems will be more intimately linked horizontally or vertically. Although discussions are under way in elementary and secondary schools, community colleges, and universities about educational problems in the United States, resulting commitments to collaboration in the areas of access, curriculum, and development might not necessarily extend to integrated indicator systems. A more likely situation would involve efforts to develop national indicators with direct links to schools and systems that would be viewed as micromanagement among lower levels of educational systems.

Performance indicator systems, however, might become more sensitive to the interdependence of all levels of education. For example, measures of students' performance in community colleges often include continuation rates to a four-year institution as a "positive" outcome (American Association of Community 1994). For K–12, the Goals 2000 Act establishes voluntary national goals in the areas of, among others, students' achievement, teachers' preparation, adult literacy, and partnerships between school and home.

Comparisons of performance could move to an international level involving multinational comparisons similar to those developed by the OECD and, more recently, by the National Center for Education Statistics (1994a). A clear movement has evolved toward developing core performance indicators that can be applied across the globe. Such measures as student outcomes, retention, time to degree, graduation, employment patterns, and continued education can be used across nations. Indeed, the indicators used by the various countries examined in this volume are comparable, thus inviting comparison if problems concerning definition are solved. Such measures could hold special promise if such measures of outcome can be adjusted for characteristics, for example, students' readiness (Astin 1993b).

Impediments to Further Development

Although performance indicators potentially can improve the quality of decision making, several obstacles to further refinement remain. First, the sheer number of indicators in some settings can serve more to confuse decision makers than to simplify the task of making choices. Winona State University, for example, tracks 250 measures (Winona 1994b), the University of Miami more than 100 (Sapp 1993; Sapp and Temares 1991, 1992). How to convert this plethora of data to information that decision makers can use remains problematic.

Second, issues of the validity and reliability of data generated from existing indicators must be addressed systematically, especially where performance indicators are part of allocating resources. Recognition is growing that quality assurance and accountability systems, such as those implied in most indicator models, cannot be designed to be applied independent of context. Institutional representatives and architects of performance systems are beginning to recognize the importance of mission and institutional context. From selecting to operationalizing indicators, decision makers are becoming more aware that context makes a difference. This heightened sensitivity has already created considerable discussion about core performance standards needed for comparison across institutions, systems, states, or countries. The problems associated with statistical or physical control of contextual variables illustrate the substantial methodological limitations that surround components of outcomes research of performance indicator initiatives (Pascarella and Terenzini 1991). Outcome measures, for example, remain a concern because of problems of "contextual validity" associated with any generic ability construct (Mentkowski and Rogers 1988).

While context remains a key factor in shaping the design of performance indicators, it is important to distinguish fiscal measures from indicators of academic process and outcomes. The language of accounting and the rules of logic that have long served measurement of fiscal accountability have nurtured a standard vocabulary within the fiscal world. Calls for sensitivity to context are more appropriate for performance accountability. Mission-driven indicator installations, such as SUNY's system and campus performance indicators, can be designed to reflect contextual factors surrounding goals for access while using business and financial measures to assess funding (Burke 1993b).

Third, as this review has shown, a leap of faith exists between concerns over input or contextual characteristics and outcomes (Nedwek 1994). This leap of faith represents the untested assumption that the educational system and its institutions, programs, or culture explain variations in outcomes.

Few signs exist that a consensus is emerging on the dimensions and indicators of process variables or the role they should play in quality assurance (U.S. Dept. of Education 1992). This lack of agreement over process measures is more apparent at the system level than at the institutional level, where public interest in the learning environment could be more focused. Equally important, at a lower level, analytic results from the use of indicators can yield more alternatives for policy. Some research, for example, has reported that what happens in the classroom is associated with cognitive growth (National Center for Higher 1993b). Opportunities for active learning, frequent feedback on performance, and peer interaction appear to influence the development of higher-order thinking skills (Astin 1993b; Light 1990; McKeachie et al. 1987). Critics of professional and regional accrediting associations in the United States note, however, that the current emphasis is on the act of assessment rather than on how the learning environment is improved (Nichols 1991a, 1991b). The irony is that while process phenomena are related to outcomes, they do require considerable investment in resources for gathering data. In addition, the methodological or political costs associated with gathering data lessen the likelihood that they will become a standard area of interest in performance indicator systems.

Process issues at the macro level have attracted recent attention through the development of proxy administrative measures. Launched in 1992, NACUBO's Benchmarking Project is one of the more ambitious attempts to apply multiple performance indicators across 38 functions and processes in higher education (Kempner and Shafer 1993). Another interesting development is the biennial survey of strategic indicators conducted by AGB in collaboration with Peterson's Guides (Taylor et al. 1991).

It is unclear whether process measures will be more widely found in performance indicator systems. We know that far more attention is currently given to outcomes and outputs. Process measures might be more useful to decision makers at the program level than to policy makers inside or outside an institution, system, or nation. The perceived utility of process measures could be more likely to increase when information serves formative evaluation goals. Sorting out the uses of indicators by various stakeholders could yield greater visibility of process measures but little integration with most existing uses of performance indicators.

Fourth, faced with the temptation of complexity, added administrative costs, resistance from faculty, and a less forgiving political culture, the probability increases that by the turn of the century most indicator systems will be viewed as too costly and ineffective as primary management tools. In the United States, for example, administrative and support costs already represent nearly 30 percent of public education expenditures (Hauptman 1990).

Fifth, in the tradition of the individualistic frontier settler, a hands-off mentality has long lingered as part of the academic culture in the United States. Despite the rituals of decisions about rank and tenure, we have held fast to the concepts of the independent, individual scholar and of academic freedom. The contribution to and responsibility for creativity in the academy have so far been largely accomplished through individual effort. Performance indicator systems do not fit the culture of individual workers well. A primary challenge for the future is to redirect institutional attention, in palatable doses, to more collective responsibility for restoring vitality and confidence in the academy. Too strong an emphasis on indicators, particularly by external agencies, however, could create an unintended backlash among faculty, reinforcing individualism at the expense of shared accountability. The resulting antagonism would likely harm the very element that such reforms seek to improve—undergraduate education.

The tension between individual accountability and collective responsibility is certainly not limited to faculty. Organizational cultures, for example, can influence administrative behavior as well (Cameron and Ettington 1988; Peterson and Spencer 1993). Reengineering higher education includes moving from external controls to individual autonomy, from centralized systems to distributed networks, from hierarchical structures to horizontal networks, and from adult-child to adult-adult professional relationships (Penrod and Dolence 1992).

Incentives to nurture a sense of collective responsibility in the culture of higher education have not been forthcoming in large doses. Whether new ways of viewing education— as interconnected and mutually dependent components of a larger system—will promote such incentives remains unclear. Current methods of funding and managing education, especially the use of distinct revenue and expenditure streams, argue against collective responsibility across educational sectors.

Sixth, despite greater technological capacity to improve the efficiency of performance indicator systems, the focus of the indicators remains an issue. Critics of indicator systems suggest that current efforts fail to develop and apply a conceptual framework that is "based on research results and the interests of policy makers and educators" (Blank 1993, p. 67). Others have argued that most indicator systems are too ambitious and unfocused and lack validity and reliability. Perhaps the best that can be said is that the technology to collect performance indicators exists, but the evaluation of the results is yet flawed.

In sum, maintaining the balance between demands for public accountability and internal quality assurance in the last half of the 1990s will not be easy. Growing pressures and a focus on centralization have created a tendency toward greater intervention by parties beyond the campus. The pace of such involvement in the early 1990s suggests yet more external influence, particularly in the United States. The necessary independence of the campus is certainly not threatened, but the same level of flexibility as in past years will be difficult

to sustain. A major objective for campus and system administrators should be to respond to the new realities and place
the institutional stamp and style on state or federal fiscal policies and education goals. The key is to strike a balance
between campus autonomy and government accountability
for all activities. To that end, the experiment is worth
continuing.

REFERENCES

The Educational Resources Information Center (ERIC) Clearinghouse on Higher Education abstracts and indexes the current literature on higher education for inclusion in ERIC's data base and announcement in ERIC's monthly bibliographic journal, *Resources in Education* (RIE). Most of these publications are available through the ERIC Document Reproduction Service (EDRS). For publications cited in this bibliography that are available from EDRS, ordering number and price code are included. Readers who wish to order a publication should write to the ERIC Document Reproduction Service, 7420 Fullerton Rd., Suite 110, Springfield, VA 22153-2852. (Phone orders with VISA or MasterCard are taken at 800-443-ERIC or 703-440-1400.) When ordering, please specify the document (ED) number. Documents are available as noted in microfiche (MF) and paper copy (PC). If you have the price code ready when you call EDRS, an exact price can be quoted. The last page of the latest issue of *Resources in Education* also has the current cost, listed by code.

Acherman, H., L. van Welie, and C. Laan. 1992. "Following up External Quality Assessments." Paper presented at the 14th Annual Forum of the European Association for Institutional Research, September, Brussels, Belgium.

Albright, Brenda N. 1984. "Effects of Enrollment, Admissions, Remediation, and Tuition Policies on Quality." In *Financial Incentives for Academic Quality,* edited by John Folger. New Directions for Higher Education No. 48. San Francisco: Jossey-Bass.

———. 1985. "Quality Incentives in the Budget." In *Making the Budget Process Work,* edited by D.J. Berg and Gerald M. Skogley. New Directions for Higher Education No. 52. San Francisco: Jossey-Bass.

———. 1994. "A Clean Slate: Principles for Moving to a Value-Driven Higher Education Funding Model." Denver: State Higher Education Executive Officers.

American Association of Community Colleges. 1994. *Community Colleges: Core Indicators of Effectiveness.* A report of the Community College Roundtable. AACC Special Reports No. 4. Washington, D.C.: Author. ED 367 411. 33 pp. MF–01; PC not available EDRS.

American Association of University Professors, Committee C. July/August 1991. "Mandated Assessment of Educational Outcomes: A Report of Committee C on College and University Teaching, Research, and Publication." *Academe:* 49–56.

Anderson, Richard, and Joel Meyerson, eds. 1992. *Productivity and Higher Education: Improving the Effectiveness of Faculty, Facilities, and Financial Resources.* Princeton, N.J.: Peterson's Guides.

Anwyl, J. 1992. *Quality in Higher Education.* Melbourne: Center for the Study of Higher Education.

Aper, Jeffery, Steven M. Cuver, and Dennis E. Hinkle. 1990. "Coming to Terms with the Accountability versus Improvement Debate in Assessment." *Higher Education* 20(4): 471–83.

Ashworth, K.H. 1994. "The Texas Case Study: Performance-Based Funding in Higher Education." *Change* 26(6): 8–15.

Association of American Colleges. 1985. *Integrity in the College Curriculum.* Washington, D.C.: Author.

Association of Commonwealth Universities. 1993. *Commonwealth Universities Yearbook.* Vol. 3. London: Author.

Association of Governing Boards. January 1994. "Ten Public Issues for Higher Education in 1994." AGB Public Policy Series No. 94-1. Washington, D.C.: Author. ED 366 236. 27 pp. MF–01; PC–02.

Association of Universities and Colleges of Canada. 1993. *Performance Indicators: Possible Roles for AUCC.* Winnipeg: Author.

Astin, Alexander W. 1982. "Why Not Try Some New Ways of Measuring Quality?" *Educational Record* 63(2): 10–15.

———. 1985. *Achieving Institutional Excellence: A Critical Assessment of Priorities and Practices in Higher Education.* San Francisco: Jossey-Bass.

———. 22 September 1993a. "College Retention Rates Are Often Misleading." *Chronicle of Higher Education:* A48.

———. 1993b. *What Matters in College?* San Francisco: Jossey-Bass.

Australian Vice Chancellors Committee/Australian Council of Directors and Principals. 1988. *Report of the AVCC/ACDP Working Party on Performance Indicators.* Canberra: Australian Government Publishing Service.

Bache, P., and P. Maassen. 1993. "Higher Education Policy in Denmark." In *Higher Education Policy: An International Comparative Perspective,* edited by L. Goedegebuure, F. Kaiser, P. Maassen, L. Meek, F. van Vught, and E. de Weert. Oxford: Pergamon Press.

Baldwin, P. 1991. *Higher Education: Quality and Diversity in the 1990s.* Canberra: Australian Government Publishing Service.

Ball, R., and J. Halwachi. 1987. "Performance Indicators in Higher Education." *Higher Education* 16: 393–405.

Ball, R., and R. Wilkinson. 1992. "The Use and Abuse of Performance Indicators in U.K. Higher Education." Paper presented at the 14th Annual Forum of the European Association for Institutional Research, September, Brussels, Belgium.

Bannister, Barry. 1991. "Valuing Academic Research: Towards a Policy for Hong Kong's Future Universities." *Assessment and Evaluation in Higher Education* 16(3): 215–24.

Banta, Trudy W. 1988. "Assessment as an Instrument of State Funding Policy." In *Implementing Outcomes Assessment: Promise and Perils.* New Directions for Institutional Research No. 59. San Francisco: Jossey-Bass.

———. 1991. "Possible Indicators of Program Effectiveness for the

University of Tennessee." Knoxville: Univ. of Tennessee, Center for Assessment, Research, and Development.

————. 1992. "Involving Faculty in Assessment." *Assessment Update* 5(1): 3–6.

————, ed. 1986. *Performance Funding in Higher Education: A Critical Analysis of Tennessee's Experience.* Boulder, Colo.: National Center for Higher Education Management Systems. ED 310 655. 176 pp. MF–01; PC–08.

Banta, Trudy W., and Homer S. Fisher. 1984. "Performance Funding: Tennessee's Experiment." In *Financial Incentives for Academic Quality,* edited by John Folger. New Directions for Higher Education No. 48. San Francisco: Jossey-Bass.

————. 1989. "Tennessee's Performance Funding Policy: L'Enfant Terrible of Assessment at Age Eight." Knoxville: Univ. of Tennessee, Center for Assessment, Research, and Development. ED 323 832. 8 pp. MF–01; PC not available EDRS.

Banta, Trudy W., and Marian S. Moffett. 1987. "Performance Funding in Tennessee: Stimulus for Program Improvement." In *Student Outcomes Assessment: What Institutions Stand to Gain,* edited by D.F. Halpern. New Directions for Higher Education No. 59. San Francisco: Jossey-Bass.

Barnett, R.A. 1989. "Quality Control and the Development of Teaching and Learning." In *Performance Indicators and Quality Control in Higher Education,* edited by M. McVicar. Portsmouth, Eng.: Portsmouth Polytechnic.

Barrett, Katherine, and Richard Greene. 1992. "How Well Run Is the Federal Government? An Open Letter to the Next President." *Financial World* 161(21): 36–81.

Barron's Educational Services. 1991. *Profiles of American Colleges.* 19th ed. Hauppauge, N.Y.: Author.

Barton, Paul. 1994. *Learning by Design.* Princeton, N.J.: Educational Testing Service.

Bateman, M., and R.W. Elliott. 1994. "An Attempt to Implement Performance-Based Funding in Texas Higher Education: A Case Study." In *Focus on the Budget: Rethinking Current Practice.* Denver: State Higher Education Executive Officers.

Bauer, M. 1990. "Sweden." In *The Development of Performance Indicators for Higher Education: A Compendium for Eleven Countries,* edited by H.R. Kells. Paris: Organization for Economic Cooperation and Development. ED 331 355. 134 pp. MF–01; PC not available EDRS.

Bennett, William J. 1984. "To Reclaim a Legacy: A Report on the Humanities in Higher Education." Washington, D.C.: National Endowment for the Humanities. ED 247 880. 63 pp. MF–01; PC–03.

————. March 1993. *Index of Leading Cultural Indicators.* Vol. 1. Washington, D.C.: Empower America.

Berdahl, Robert O., and Barbara A. Holland, eds. 1990. *Developing State Fiscal Incentives to Improve Higher Education.* College Park, Md.: National Center for Postsecondary Governance and Finance.

Berdahl, Robert O., and Susan M. Studds. 1990. "The Selective Enhancement of Quality Education: The Tension between Excellence and Equity." In *Developing State Fiscal Incentives to Improve Higher Education,* edited by Robert O. Berdahl and Barbara A. Holland. College Park, Md.: National Center for Postsecondary Governance and Finance.

Blank, Rolf K. 1993. "Developing a System of Education Indicators: Selecting, Implementing, and Reporting Indicators." *Educational Evaluation and Policy Analysis* 15(1): 65–80.

Bleakley, Fred R. 6 July 1993. "The Best Laid Plans: Many Companies Try Management Fads, Only to See Them Flop." *Wall Street Journal.*

Bloom, Allan. 1987. *The Closing of the American Mind.* New York: Simon & Schuster.

Blumenstyk, Goldie. 1 September 1993. "Colleges Look to 'Benchmarking' to Measure How Efficient and Productive They Are." *Chronicle of Higher Education.*

Blumenstyk, Goldie, and Mary Crystal Cage. 9 January 1991. "Public Colleges Expect Financial Hardship in 1991, as Budget Crises Imperil State Appropriations." *Chronicle of Higher Education* 37(17): A1+.

Bogue, E. Grady. 1982. "Allocation of Public Funds on Instructional Performance/Quality Indicators." *International Journal of Institutional Management in Higher Education* 6(1): 23–27.

———. 1993. "The Effectiveness of State-Level Policies Related to Quality, Performance, and Accountability." Paper presented to a meeting of the Society for College and University Planning, Boston, Massachusetts.

Bogue, E. Grady, and Wayne Brown. 1982. "Performance Incentives for State Colleges: How Tennessee Is Trying to Improve the Return on Its Higher Education." *Harvard Business Review* 60(6): 123–28.

Bogue, E. Grady, Joseph Creech, and John Folger. 1993. *Assessing Quality in Higher Education: Policy Actions in the SREB States.* Atlanta: Southern Regional Education Board.

Bogue, E. Grady, and R.L. Saunders. 1992. *The Evidence for Quality.* San Francisco: Jossey-Bass.

Bok, Derek. 1986. *Higher Learning.* London: Harvard Univ. Press.

Borden, Victor M.H., and Trudy Banta. 1994. "Performance Indicators for Accountability and Improvement." In *Using Performance Indicators to Guide Strategic Decision Making,* edited by Victor M.H. Borden and Trudy Banta. New Directions for Institutional Research No. 82. San Francisco: Jossey-Bass.

Borden, Victor M.H., and K.V. Bottrill. 1994. "Performance Indicators:

History, Definitions, and Methods." In *Using Performance Indicators to Guide Strategic Decision Making*, edited by Victor M.H. Borden and Trudy Banta. New Directions for Institutional Research No. 82. San Francisco: Jossey Bass.

Borman, J.J. 1987. "The Role of Performance Indicators in Improving the Dialogue between Government and Universities." *International Journal of Institutional Management in Higher Education* 11(2): 181–94.

Bormans, M., R. Brouwer, F. Dochy, O. McDaniel, F. Mertens, C. Paardekooper, M. Seegers, A. Spee, H. Tseng, R. Veld, and W. Wijnen. 1990. "Netherlands." In *The Development of Performance Indicators for Higher Education: A Compendium for Eleven Countries*, edited by H.R. Kells. Paris: Organization for Economic Cooperation and Development. ED 331 355. 134 pp. MF–01; PC not available EDRS.

Bottani, Norberto, and Isabelle Delfau. February/March 1990. "The Search for International Education Indicators." *OECD Observer* 162: 14–18.

Bottrill, K.V., and V.M.H. Borden. 1994. "Appendix: Examples from the Literature." In *Using Performance Indicators to Guide Strategic Decision Making*, edited by V.M.H. Borden and T.W. Banta. New Directions for Institutional Research No. 82. San Francisco: Jossey-Bass.

Bourke, P. 1986. *Quality Measures in Universities*. Canberra: Commonwealth Tertiary Education Commission.

Bowen, Howard R. 1974. *The Products of Higher Education*. New Directions for Institutional Research. San Francisco: Jossey-Bass.

———. 1977. *Investment in Learning: The Individual and Social Value of American Higher Education*. San Francisco: Jossey-Bass.

Boyer, Carol M., and Aims C. McGuinness, Jr. February 1986. "State Initiatives to Improve Undergraduate Education, ECS Survey Highlights." *AAHE Bulletin:* 3–7.

Boyer, Carol M., et al. 1986. "Transforming the State Role in Undergraduate Education: Time for a Different View." Denver: Education Commission of the States. ED 275 219. 45 pp. MF–01; PC not available EDRS.

Boyer, Ernest L. 1987. *College: The Undergraduate Experience in America*. New York: Harper & Row.

———. 1990. *Scholarship Reconsidered: Priorities of the Professorate*. Princeton, N.J.: Carnegie Foundation for the Advancement of Teaching. ED 326 149. 151 pp. MF–01; PC not available EDRS.

Brennan, J. 1990. "Quality Assessment in the Public Sector in Great Britain." In *Peer Review and Performance Indicators: Quality Assessment in British and Dutch Higher Education*, edited by L. Goedegebuure, P. Maassen, and D. Westerheijden. Utrecht: Uitgeverij Lemma B.V.

Brinkman, Paul. 1982. *State Funding of Public Higher Education: Improving the Practice.* Boulder, Colo.: National Center for Higher Education Management Systems. ED 246 813. 46 pp. MF–01; PC–02.

Burke, Joseph C. 1993a. "Meeting the Productivity Challenge: System Performance Reports." Studies in Public Higher Education No. 4. Albany: State Univ. of New York, Office of the Chancellor.

———. 1993b. "Preserving Quality while Enhancing Productivity." Studies in Higher Education No. 4. Albany: State Univ. of New York, Office of the Provost.

———. May 1994. "Assessment: Vision's the Thing." In *Faculty Perspectives: Sharing Ideas on Assessment.* Albany: State Univ. of New York, Faculty Senate.

Cage, Mary Crystal. 20 April 1994. "End to Recession's Chill?" *Chronicle of Higher Education* 40(33): A19–24.

California State University. 1989. "Student Outcomes Assessment in the California State University." Long Beach: Advisory Committee on Student Outcomes Assessment.

Cameron, Kim S., and D. Ettington. 1988. "The Conceptual Foundations of Organizational Culture." In *Higher Education: Handbook of Theory and Research,* edited by J.C. Smart. Vol. 4. New York: Agathon Press.

Cameron, Kim S., and Mary Tschirhart. 1992. "Post-Industrial Environments and Organizational Effectiveness in Colleges and Universities." *Journal of Higher Education* 63(1): 87–108.

Camp, Robert C. 1989. *Benchmarking: The Search for Industry Best Practices that Lead to Superior Performance.* Milwaukee: ASQS Quality Press.

Canadian Education Statistics Council. 1992. *A Statistical Portrait of University-Level Education in Canada.* Ottawa: Author.

Cave, M., S. Hanney, and M. Kogan. 1991. *The Use of Performance Indicators in Higher Education: A Critical Analysis of Developing Practice.* 2d ed. London: Jessica Kingsley Publishers.

Cave, M., M. Kogan, and S. Hanney. 1990. "The Scope and Effects of Performance Measurement in British Higher Education." In *Management Information and Performance Indicators in Higher Education: An International Issue,* edited by F. Dochy, M. Segers, and W. Wijnen. Assen, the Netherlands: Van Gorcum & Co.

Chabotar, K.J. 1989. "Financial Ratio Analysis Comes to Nonprofits." *Journal of Higher Education* 60(2): 188–208.

Chaffee, E., and L. Sherr. 1992. *Quality: Transforming Postsecondary Education.* ASHE-ERIC Higher Education Report No. 3. Washington, D.C.: George Washington Univ., School of Education and Human Development. ED 351 922. 145 pp. MF–01; PC–06.

Chickering, A.W., and Z.F. Gamson. 1987. "Seven Principles for Good Practice in Undergraduate Education." *AAHE Bulletin* 39(7): 3–7.

Chronicle of Higher Education. 21 August 1992. "Almanac."

Clowes, Darrel A. 1992. "Remediation in American Higher Education." In *Higher Education: Handbook of Theory and Research,* edited by John C. Smart. Vol. 8. New York: Agathon Press.

Commission of Inquiry on Canadian University Education. 1991. "Report." Ottawa: Association of Universities and Colleges of Canada.

Commission on Institutions of Higher Education, and North Central Association of Colleges and Schools. 1991. "Statement on Assessment and Student Academic Achievement." *NCA Quarterly* 66(2): 393.

————. 1993. *Handbook of Accreditation: 1993–94.* Working Draft. Chicago: Commission on Institutions of Higher Education.

Committee of Vice Chancellors and Principals. 1985. "Report of the Steering Committee for Efficiency Studies in Universities." Jarratt Report. London: Author.

Committee of Vice Chancellors and Principals, and Universities Funding Council. 1990. *University Management Statistics and Performance Indicators in the U.K.* 4th ed. London: Author.

Committee of Vice Chancellors and Principals, and University Grants Committee. 1986. *Performance Indicators in Universities: A First Statement by a Joint CVCP/UGC Working Group.* London: Committee of Vice Chancellors and Principals.

Commonwealth Tertiary Education Commission. 1989. *Review of Efficiency and Effectiveness in Higher Education: Report of a Committee of Enquiry.* Canberra: Australian Government Publishing Service.

Conference of Rectors and Principals of Quebec Universities. 1991. *Universities: A Reflection of Quebec Society.* Montreal: Author.

Coordinating Board for Higher Education. 1992. "Task Force on Critical Choices for Higher Education." Jefferson City, Mo.: Author.

Crosby, P. 1979. *Quality Is Free.* New York: McGraw-Hill.

Cuenin, S. 1987. "The Use of Performance Indicators in Universities: An International Survey." *International Journal of Institutional Management in Higher Education* 11(2): 117–39.

Cullen, B. 1987. "Performance Indicators in U.K. Higher Education: Progress and Prospects." *International Journal of Institutional Management in Higher Education* 11(2): 171–80.

Cunningham, Stephanie. February 1993. "1992 Student Assessment Report." Denver: Colorado Commission on Higher Education.

Darling-Hammond, Linda. 1992. "Educational Indicators and Enlightened Policy." *Educational Policy* 6(3): 235–65.

De Jager, G. 1992. "Using Cost Measures as Performance Indicators: The Cost Configuration Approach." Paper presented at the 14th Annual Forum of the European Association for Institutional Research, September, Brussels, Belgium.

Deming, W. 1986. *Out of the Crisis.* Cambridge: Massachusetts Institute of Technology.

Department of Education and Science. 1991. *Higher Education: A New Framework.* London: HMSO.

"The Development of Higher Education into the 1990s." 1985. Green Paper. London: HMSO.

de Weert, E. 1990. "A Macro-analysis of Quality Assessment in Higher Education." *Higher Education* 19: 57–72.

De Young, Alan J. 1985. "Assessing 'Faculty Productivity' in Colleges of Education: Penetration of the Technical Thesis into the Status System of Academe." *Educational Theory* 35(4): 411–21.

Diamond, Robert M., and Bronwyn E. Adam, eds. 1993. *Recognizing Faculty Work: Reward Systems for the Year 2000.* New Directions for Higher Education No. 81. San Francisco: Jossey-Bass.

Dill, David. 1992. "Quality by Design: Toward a Framework for Academic Quality Management." In *Higher Education: Handbook of Theory and Research.* Vol. 8. New York: Agathon Press.

DiSalvo, P. 1989. "Ratio Analysis in Higher Education: Caveat Emptor." *Journal of Education Finance* 14: 500–12.

Dochy, F., and M. Segers. 1990. "Selecting Indicators on the Basis of Essential Criteria and Appropriate Assessment Methods for a Quality Assurance System." Paper prepared for a CHEPS conference, Quality Assessment in Higher Education, March, Utrecht, the Netherlands.

Dochy, F., M. Segers, and W. Wijnen. 1990a. "Preliminaries to the Implementation of a Quality Assurance System Based on Management Information and Performance Indicators: Results of a Validity Study." In *Management Information and Performance Indicators in Higher Education: An International Issue,* edited by F. Dochy, M. Segers, and W. Wijnen. Assen, the Netherlands: Van Gorcum & Co.

———. 1990b. "Selecting Performance Indicators: A Proposal as a Result of Research." In *Peer Review and Performance Indicators: Quality Assessment in British and Dutch Higher Education,* edited by L. Goedegebuure, P. Maassen, and D. Westerheijden. Utrect: Uitgeverij Lemma B.V.

Dodge, Susan. 4 December 1991. "Slashed Budgets Force Students to Delay Graduation Plans and Change Majors." *Chronicle of Higher Education* 38(15): A1.

Dooris, Michael J., and Deborah J. Teeter. 1994. "Total Quality Management Perspective on Assessing Institutional Performance." In *Using Performance Indicators to Guide Strategic Decision Making,* edited by Victor M.H. Borden and Trudy Banta. New Directions for Institutional Research No. 82. San Francisco: Jossey-Bass.

Doucette, D., and B. Hughes, eds. 1993. *Assessing Institutional Effectiveness in Community Colleges.* Laguna Hills, Calif.: League for Innovation in the Community College.

Doyle, K. 1994. "Integrating Performance Measurement and Quality Assurance in the University Planning Process: A Case Study of the University of Technology, Sydney." Paper presented at the 16th Annual EAIR Forum, August 21-24, Amsterdam.

Drenth, P., W. Van Os, and G. Bernaert. 1989. "Improvement of Education through Internal Evaluation (AMOS)." In *Evaluating Higher Education,* edited by M. Kogan. London: Jessica Kingsley Publishers.

Dubin, Robert, and Thomas Taveggia. 1968. *The Teaching-Learning Paradox: A Comparative Analysis of College Teaching Methods.* Eugene: Univ. of Oregon, Center for the Advanced Study of Educational Administration. ED 026 966. 85 pp. MF–01; PC–04.

Dumont, Richard G. 1980. "Performance Funding and Power Relations in Higher Education." *Journal of Higher Education* 51(4): 400-23.

Eash, Maurice. 1983. "Educational Research Productivity of Institutions of Higher Education." *American Educational Research Journal* 20(1): 5-12.

Eccles, Robert. January/February 1991. "The Performance Measurement Manifesto." *Harvard Business Review* 69: 131-37.

Edgerton, Russell. December 1991. "National Standards Are Coming! . . . National Standards Are Coming!" *AAHE Bulletin:* 8-12.

———. 1993a. "The Reexamination of Faculty Priorities." *Change* 25(4): 16.

———. 1993b. "The Tasks Faculty Perform." *Change* 25(4): 4-6.

Education Commission of the States. 1990. *Assessment and Accountability in Higher Education.* ECS Proceedings Document. Washington, D.C.: Author. ED 321 703. 32 pp. MF–01; PC–02.

Elton, L. November 1987. "Warning Signs." *Times Higher Education Supplement* 9. London.

———. 1988. "A Review of [Cave, Hanney, Kogan, and Trevett's] 'The Use of Performance Indicators in Higher Education: A Critical Analysis of Developing Practice.'" *Studies in Higher Education* 13(3): 337-38.

The Europa World Year Book. 1993. Vol. 2. London: Europa Publications Ltd.

Evangelauf, Jean. 30 July 1986. "National Reports on Undergraduate Education Spur Changes at One in Three Colleges, Survey Finds." *Chronicle of Higher Education* 32: 1+.

Ewell, Peter T. 1985. "Assessment: What's It All About?" *Change* 17(6): 32-36.

———. 1987. "Assessment, Accountability, and Improvement: Managing the Contradiction." Paper presented at the Second National Conference on Assessment of the American Association for Higher Education, Boulder, Colorado. ED 287 330. 25 pp. MF–01; PC–01.

———. 1989. "Information for Decision: What's the Use?" In

Enhancing Information Use in Decision Making, edited by P.T. Ewell. New Directions for Institutional Research No. 64. San Francisco: Jossey-Bass.

———. 1990. "Assessment and 'New Accountability': A Challenge for Higher Education's Leadership." Denver: Education Commission of the States. ED 321 702. 26 pp. MF–01; PC–02.

———. 1991. "Assessment and Public Accountability: Back to the Future." *Change* 23(6): 12–17.

———. 1992a. "Feeling the Elephant: The Quest to Capture 'Quality.'" *Change* 24(5): 44–47.

———. 1992b. "Outcomes Assessment, Institutional Effectiveness, and Accreditation: A Conceptual Exploration in Accreditation, Assessment, and Institutional Effectiveness." Resource papers for the COPA Task Force on Institutional Effectiveness. Washington, D.C.: COPA.

———. 1993a. "Performance Indicators: A New Round of Accountability." *Assessment Update* 5(3): 12.

———. 1993b. "A Preliminary Study of the Feasibility and Utility for National Policy on Instructional 'Good Practice' Indicators in Undergraduate Education." Boulder, Colo.: National Center for Higher Education Management Systems.

———. 1994a. "Developing Statewide Performance Indicators for Higher Education: Policy Themes and Variations." In *Charting Higher Education Accountability: A Sourcebook on State-Level Performance Indicators,* edited by Sandra S. Ruppert. Denver: Education Commission of the States. ED 375 789. 177 pp. MF–01; PC–08.

———. 1994b. "Developing Statewide Performance Indicators for Higher Education: Policy Themes and Variations." ECS Working Papers (Draft). Denver: Education Commission of the States.

———. March 1994c. "Indicators of 'Good Practice': New Tools for New Times." *NCHEMS News* 9: 2–3.

———. 1994d. Remarks before a North Central Association annual meeting, March 27, Chicago, Illinois.

———. 1994e. "Tennessee." In *Charting Higher Education Accountability: A Sourcebook on State-Level Performance Indicators,* edited by Sandra S. Ruppert. Denver: Education Commission of the States. ED 375 789. 177 pp. MF–01; PC–08.

———. 1994f. "Tennessee." ECS Working Papers (Draft). Denver: Education Commission of the States.

———. 1994g. "Virginia." In *Charting Higher Education Accountability: A Sourcebook on State-Level Performance Indicators,* edited by Sandra S. Ruppert. Denver: Education Commission of the States. ED 375 789. 177 pp. MF–01; PC–08.

———. 1994h. "Virginia." ECS Working Papers (Draft). Denver: Education Commission of the States.

————. 1994i. "Wisconsin." In *Charting Higher Education Account-ability: A Sourcebook on State-Level Performance Indicators,* edited by Sandra S. Ruppert. Denver: Education Commission of the States. ED 375 789. 177 pp. MF–01; PC–08.

————. 1994j. "Wisconsin." ECS Working Papers (Draft). Denver: Education Commission of the States.

Ewell, Peter T., John Finney, and Charles Lenth. 1990. "Filling in the Mosaic: The Emerging Pattern of State-Based Assessment." *AAHE Bulletin* 42(8): 3–5.

Ewell, Peter T., and Dennis P. Jones. 1991. *Actions Matter: The Case for Indirect Measures in Assessing Higher Education's Progress on the National Education Goals.* Boulder, Colo.: National Center for Higher Education Management Systems. ED 340 756. 55 pp. MF–01; PC–03.

————. 1994. "Pointing the Way: Indicators as Policy Tools in Higher Education." In *Charting Higher Education Accountability: A Sourcebook on State-Level Performance Indicators,* edited by Sandra S. Ruppert. Denver: Education Commission of the States. ED 375 789. 177 pp. MF–01; PC–08.

Eyler, Janet. 1984. "The Politics of Quality in Higher Education." In *Financial Incentives for Academic Quality,* edited by John Folger. New Directions for Higher Education No. 48. San Francisco: Jossey-Bass.

Federal Register. 8 September 1987. "Secretary's Procedures and Criteria for Recognition of Accrediting Agencies." Proposed Rules 52(173): 33908–13. Washington, D.C.: U.S. Government Printing Office.

————. 29 April 1994a. "Secretary's Procedures and Criteria for Recognition of Accrediting Agencies." 2d release. Proposed Rules 59(82): 3578, 12881. Washington, D.C.: U.S. Government Printing Office.

————. 29 April 1994b. *State Postsecondary Review Program.* Final Rule 59(82): 22286–321. Washington, D.C.: U.S. Government Printing Office.

Feldman, Kenneth. 1983. "Seniority and Experience of College Teachers as Related to Evaluations They Receive from Students." *Research in Higher Education* 18(1): 3–122.

Findlay, P. 1990. "Developments in the Performance Indicator Debate in the United Kingdom." In *Peer Review and Performance Indicators: Quality Assessment in British and Dutch Higher Education,* edited by L. Goedegebuure, P. Maassen, and D. Westerheijden. Utrecht: Uitgeverij Lemma B.V.

Florida State Postsecondary Education Planning Commission. 19 April 1990. "The Impact of Undergraduate Enhancement Funding." Report No. 7. ED 319 324. 82 pp. MF–01; PC–04.

————. March 1992. "Outcomes Assessment in Postsecondary Education." Report No. 5. ED 344 559. 49 pp. MF–01; PC–02.

Folger, John. 1984a. "Assessment of Quality for Accountability." In *Financial Incentives for Academic Quality,* edited by John Folger. New Directions for Higher Education No. 48. San Francisco: Jossey-Bass.

———, ed. 1984b. *Financial Incentives for Academic Quality.* New Directions for Higher Education No. 48. San Francisco: Jossey-Bass.

———. 1990. "Designing State Incentive Programs That Work in Higher Education." In *Developing State Fiscal Incentives to Improve Higher Education.* College Park, Md.: National Center for Postsecondary Governance and Finance.

Folger, John, and Dennis Jones. 1993. *Using Fiscal Policy to Achieve State Education Goals: State Policy and College Learning.* Denver: Education Commission of the States. ED 366 242. 44 pp. MF–01; PC–02.

Forum for College and University Governance. 1990. *State Incentive Funding: Leveraging Quality.* Briefings. College Park: Univ. of Maryland.

Frackmann, E. 1987. "Lessons to Be Learnt from a Decade of Discussions on Performance Indicators." *International Journal of Institutional Management in Higher Education* 11(2): 149–62.

Frances, C., G. Huxel, J. Meyerson, and D. Park. 1987. *Strategic Decision Making: Key Questions and Indicators for Trustees.* Washington, D.C.: Association of Governing Boards of Universities and Colleges.

Frantz, Alan C. 1992. "Mandated Accountability in Colorado Higher Education: House Bill 1187, 1985 to 1991." Paper presented at an annual meeting of the American Education Research Association, April 20, Denver, Colorado. ED 347 932. 43 pp. MF–01; PC–02.

Frederiks, M.M.H., D.F. Westerheijden, and P.J.M. Weusthof. 1994. "Effects of Quality Assessment in Dutch Higher Education." *Education Journal of Education* 29: 181–99.

Fuchsberg, Gilbert. 24 November 1993a. "Baldrige Awards to Add Schools and Hospitals." *Wall Street Journal.*

———. 1 October 1993b. "Why Shake-ups Work for Some, Not for Others." *Wall Street Journal.*

Furumart, A.M. 1989. "Institutional Self-Evaluation in Sweden." In *Evaluating Higher Education,* edited by M. Kogan. London: Jessica Kingsley Publishers.

Gaff, Jerry G. 1991. *New Life for the College Curriculum: Assessing Achievements and Furthering Progress in the Reform of General Education.* San Francisco: Jossey-Bass.

Gaither, Gerald. 1993. "Performance Funding in Texas." *Assessment Update* 5(42): 12–13.

Gallagher, A. 1991. "Comparative Value Added as a Performance Indicator." *Higher Education Review* 23(3): 19–29.

Garver, Roger C., and Dick Lucore. 1993. "The Failure of TQM." *Planning Forum* 6(7): 7.

Gehl, J. 1992. "How to Count a Computer." *EDUCOM Review* 27(6): 18.

Gill, Judith, and Laura Saunders, eds. 1992. *Developing Effective Policy Analysis in Higher Education.* New Directions for Institutional Research No. 76. San Francisco: Jossey-Bass.

Goedegebuure, L., F. Kaiser, P. Maassen, and E. de Weert. 1993. "Higher Education Policy in the Netherlands." In *Higher Education Policy: An International Comparative Perspective,* edited by L. Goedegebuure, F. Kaiser, P. Maassen, L. Meek, F. van Vught, and E. de Weert. Oxford: Pergamon Press.

Goedegebuure, L.C., P. Maassen, and D. Westerheijden. 1990a. "Quality Assessment in Higher Education." In *Peer Review and Performance Indicators: Quality Assessment in British and Dutch Higher Education,* edited by L. Goedegebuure, P. Maassen, and D. Westerheijden. Utrecht: Uitgeverij Lemma B.V.

———, eds. 1990b. *Peer Review and Performance Indicators: Quality Assessment in British and Dutch Higher Education.* Utrecht: Uitgeverij Lemma B.V.

Goedegebuure, L., and V.L. Meek. 1989. "The Restructuring of Higher Education: A Comparison of Australian and Dutch Developments." In *Towards Excellence in European Higher Education in the Nineties,* edited by E. Frackmann and P. Maassen. Utrecht: Uitgeverij Lemma B.V.

Gordon, George. 1991. "The Universities and Performance Indicators." Proceedings of a seminar held at Glasgow Polytechnic, September. Glasgow: Scottish Centrally Funded Colleges.

———. 1992. "Quality Audit and Quality Assessment." Paper presented at the 14th Annual Forum of the European Association for Institutional Research, September, Vrije Universiteit, Brussels, Belgium.

Gould, E. 1992. "Enlivening the Self-Study Process: The Coordinator's Role." A collection of papers on self-study and institutional improvement. Chicago: North Central Association of Colleges and Schools.

Grassmuck, Karen. 14 August 1991. "Throughout the 80s, Colleges Hired More Nonteaching Staff than Other Employees." *Chronicle of Higher Education* 37: A22.

Gray, James. 1951. *The University of Minnesota at Minneapolis, 1851–1951.* Minneapolis: Univ. of Minnesota Press.

Green, Diana, ed. 1994. *What Is Quality in Higher Education?* Buckingham, Eng.: Society for Research into Higher Education and Open University Press.

Green, Joslyn. 1984. "Catalog of Changes." In *Incentives for Quality and Management Flexibility in Higher Education.* Denver: Education Commission of the States. ED 255 164. 73 pp. MF–01; PC–03.

Grigg, L., and P. Sheehan. 1989. *Evaluating Research: The Role of Performance Indicators.* St. Lucia: Univ. of Queensland.

Hairston, Elaine H. 1990. "State Fiscal Incentives in Higher Education: Ohio's Selective Excellence Program." In *Developing State Fiscal Incentives to Improve Higher Education.* College Park, Md.: National Center for Postsecondary Governance and Finance.

Hanson, Gary. 1992. "Using Multiple Program Impact Analysis to Document Institutional Effectiveness." Paper presented at a forum of the Association for Institutional Research, Atlanta, Georgia.

Harder, Martha. 1981. *Faculty Productivity in Colleges/Schools of Teacher Education.* ED 212 558. 43 pp. MF–01; PC–02.

Harman, G. 1994. "Australian Higher Education Administration and the Quality Assurance Movement." *Journal of Tertiary Education Administration* 16(1): 25–43.

Harris, D., and F. Dochy. 1990. "Theoretical Considerations and Practical Pitfalls: The Use of Performance Indicators." In *Management Information and Performance Indicators in Higher Education: An International Issue,* edited by F. Dochy, M. Segers, and W. Wijnen. Assen, the Netherlands: Van Gorcum & Co.

Hattie, J. 1990. "Performance Indicators in Education." *Australian Journal of Education* 34(3): 249–76.

Hauptman, A.M. 1990. *The College Tuition Spiral: An Examination of Why Charges Are Increasing.* Washington, D.C.: American Council on Education. ED 320 502. 120 pp. MF–01; PC not available EDRS.

Hawkins, S. 1990. "Canada." In *The Development of Performance Indicators for Higher Education: A Compendium for Eleven Countries,* edited by H.R. Kells. Paris: Organization for Economic Cooperation and Development. ED 331 355. 134 pp. MF–01; PC not available EDRS.

Henry, Tamara. 9 September 1993. "90 Million Can Barely Read, Write." *USA Today.*

Heydinger, Richard B., and Hasan Simsek. 1992. *An Agenda for Reshaping Faculty Productivity.* Denver: State Higher Education Executive Officers/Education Commission of the States. ED 356 727. 38 pp. MF–01; PC–02.

Higher Education Council. 1992. *The Quality of Higher Education.* Discussion papers. Canberra: Australian Government Publishing Service.

Higher Education Funding Council for England. 1993. *Higher Education Funding, 1993–94.* Circular 2/93. Bristol, Eng.: Author.

Higher Education: A Policy Statement. 1988. Canberra: Australian Government Publishing Service.

Hodgkinson, Harold L. March 1981. "Beyond Productivity to Quality." Submitted to *AAHE Bulletin.* ED 207 385. 9 pp. MF–01; PC–01.

Holland, Barbara A. 1990. "State Incentive Funding: Leveraging Quality." College Park, Md.: National Center for Postsecondary Governance and Finance. ED 319 294. 7 pp. MF–01; PC–01.

Holland, Barbara A., and Robert O. Berdahl. 1990. "Green Carrots: A Survey of State Use of Fiscal Incentives for Academic Quality." Paper presented at an annual meeting of the Association for the Study of Higher Education, November, Washington, D.C. ED 326 131. 24 pp. MF–01; PC–01.

Hollander, T. Edward. Spring 1991. "States and College Reform: New Jersey's Experiment." *Planning for Higher Education* 19: 25–31.

Hollins, Carol S. 1992. *Containing Costs and Improving Productivity in Higher Education.* New Directions for Institutional Research No. 75. San Francisco: Jossey-Bass.

Hölttä, S. 1988. "Recent Changes in the Finnish Higher Education System." *European Journal of Education* 23(1/2): 91–103.

Howard, R., G. McLaughlin, and J. McLaughlin. 1989. "Bridging the Gap between the Data Base and User in a Distributed Environment." *Cause/Effect* 2(2): 19–25.

Howell, Nancy. 1987. "A Comparative Analysis of Higher Education Incentive Funding Methods Used in 12 States." E.D. dissertation, Univ. of Tennessee.

Huber, Richard M. November 1992. "Why Not Run a College like a Business?" *Across the Board:* 28–32.

Hüfner, Klaus. 1987a. "Differentiation and Competition in Higher Education: Recent Trends in the Federal Republic of Germany." *European Journal of Education* 22(2): 133–43.

———. 1987b. "The Role of Performance Indicators in Higher Education: The Case of Germany." *International Journal of Institutional Management in Higher Education* 11(2): 140–48.

Hüfner, Klaus, and Einhard Rau. 1987. "Excellence in Higher Education. Measuring Performance in Higher Education: Problems and Perspectives." *Higher Education in Europe* 12(4): 5–13.

Hutchings, P. 1989. "Behind Outcomes: Contexts and Questions for Assessment." Resource paper for an American Association for Higher Education Assessment Forum, June, Washington, D.C. ED 311 777. 31 pp. MF–01; PC–02.

———. 1991. "Learning over Time: Portfolio Assessment." *AAHE Bulletin* 42(8): 6–8.

Hutchings, P., and T. Marchese. 1990. "Watching Assessment: Questions, Stories, Prospects." *Change* 22(4): 12–38.

Huxel, F.C., J. Meyerson, and D. Park. 1987. *Strategic Decision Making: Key Questions and Indicators for Trustees.* Washington, D.C.: Association of Governing Boards of Universities and Colleges. ED 293 424. 96 pp. MF–01; PC–04.

Hyatt, James A., and Aurora A. Santiago. 1984. *Incentives and Disincentives for Effective Management.* Washington, D.C.: National Association of College and University Business Officers. ED 257

347. 66 pp. MF–01; PC not available EDRS.

Hyde, William. 1983. "Improving Higher Education through Budget Incentives." ECS Issuegram No. 21. Denver: Education Commission of the States. ED 234 667. 10 pp. MF–01; PC–01.

Jacobi, M., A. Astin, and F. Ayala, Jr. 1987. *College Student Outcomes Assessment: A Talent Development Perspective.* ASHE-ERIC Higher Education Report No. 7. Washington, D.C.: Association for the Study of Higher Education. ED 296 693. 141 pp. MF–01; PC–06.

Jacobson, Robert L. 15 April 1992. "More Time in the Classroom: Colleges Face New Pressure to Increase Faculty Productivity." *Chronicle of Higher Education* 38(32): A1+.

Jalongo, Mary R. 1985. "Faculty Productivity in Higher Education." *Education Forum* 49(2): 171–82.

Johansson, T. 1990. "Norway." In *The Development of Performance Indicators for Higher Education: A Compendium for Eleven Countries,* edited by H.R. Kells. Paris: Organization for Economic Cooperation and Development. ED 331 355. 134 pp. MF–01; PC not available EDRS.

Johnes, Jill, and Jim Taylor. 1990. *Performance Indicators in Higher Education.* Buckingham, Eng.: Society for Research into Higher Education/Open University Press.

Johnstone, D. Bruce. 1993a. "Enhancing the Productivity of Learning." *AAHE Bulletin:* 3–8.

———. 1993b. *Learning Productivity: A New Imperative for American Higher Education.* Studies in Public Education No. 3. Albany: State Univ. of New York. ED 357 721. 32 pp. MF–01; PC–02.

Jones, Dennis P. 1984. "Budgeting for Academic Quality: Structures and Strategies." In *Financial Incentives for Academic Quality,* edited by John Folger. New Directions for Higher Education No. 48. San Francisco: Jossey-Bass.

Jones, Dennis P., and Peter T. Ewell. 1993a. "Pointing the Way: Indicators as Policy Tools in Higher Education." ECS Working Papers (Draft). Denver: Education Commission of the States.

———. 1993b. "State-Level Indicators of Higher Education: A Conceptual Framework with Particular Applications to the Improvement of Undergraduate Study." ECS Working Papers (Draft). Denver: Education Commission of the States.

Jones, Glen A. 1989. "Keeping Legislators Informed: The University of Manitoba Study." ED 313 983. 26 pp. MF–01; PC–02.

Jongbloed, B.W.A., and D.E. Westerheijden. 1994. "Performance Indicators and Quality Assessment in European Higher Education." In *Using Performance Indicators to Guide Strategic Decision Making,* edited by Victor M.H. Borden and Trudy W. Banta. New Directions for Institutional Research No. 82. San Francisco: Jossey-Bass.

Jordan, Stephen, and Daniel Layzell. 1992. *A Case Study of Faculty Workload Issues in Arizona: Implications for State Higher Edu-*

cation Policy. Denver: State Higher Education Executive Officers/ Education Commission of the States. ED 356 729. 32 pp. MF–01; PC–02.

Kalecki, J. 1990. "A Government Perspective on Quality Assessment in Dutch Higher Education." In *Peer Review and Performance Indicators: Quality Assessment in British and Dutch Higher Education,* edited by L. Goedegebuure, P. Maassen, and D. Westerheijden. Utrecht: Uitgeverij Lemma B.V.

Kalsbeek, D. 1991. "Exploring Information as a User Construct: Case Studies of Information Use in the Policy Process." Ph.D. dissertation, St. Louis Univ.

Katz, R.N., and R.P. West. 1992. *Sustaining Excellence in the 21st Century: A Vision and Strategies for College and University Administration.* Professional Paper No. 8. Boulder, Colo.: Association for the Management of Information Technology in Higher Education. ED 355 843. 31 pp. MF–01; PC–02.

Kells, H.R. 1990. "Quality Assessment in European Higher Education." In *Peer Review and Performance Indicators: Quality Assessment in British and Dutch Higher Education,* edited by L. Goedegebuure, P. Maassen, and D. Westerheijden. Utrecht: Uitgeverij Lemma B.V.

———. 1992a. "An Analysis of the Nature and Recent Development of Performance Indicators in Higher Education." *Higher Education Management* 4(2): 131–38.

———. 1992b. *Performance Indicators for Higher Education: A Critical Review with Policy Recommendations.* PHREE Background Paper Series No. PHREE/92/56. World Bank.

———, ed. 1993. *The Development of Performance Indicators for Higher Education: A Compendium for Eleven Countries.* 2d ed. Paris: Organization for Economic Cooperation and Development. ED 331 355. 134 pp. MF–01; PC not available EDRS.

Kempner, D., and B. Shafer. 1993. "NACUBO Benchmarking: New Perspectives." *NAC Article 1193:* 1–21.

Kennedy, Paul. 1993. *Preparing for the Twenty-First Century.* New York: Random House.

Kogan, Maurice. 1989. "The Evaluation of Higher Education: An Introductory Note." In *Evaluating Higher Education,* edited by M. Kogan. London: Jessica Kingsley Publishers.

Kogan, M., and D. Kogan. 1983. *The Attack on Higher Education.* London: Kogan Page Ltd.

Konrad, Alison M. 1991. "Faculty Productivity and Demographics." *NEA Higher Education Journal* 7(2): 19–54.

KPMG Peat Marwick. 1990. *Ratio Analysis in Higher Education.* 2d ed. New York: Author.

Lasher, William F., and Deborah L. Greene. 1993. "College and University Budgeting: What Do We Know? What Do We Need to

Know?" In *Higher Education: Handbook of Theory and Research,* edited by John C. Smart. Vol. 9. New York: Agathon Press.

Lavin, Douglas. 4 October 1993. "Robert Eaton Thinks 'Vision' Is Overrated and He's Not Alone." *Wall Street Journal.*

Lawrence, G. Ben, and Allan L. Service, eds. 1977. *Quantitative Approaches to Higher Education Management: Potential, Limits, and Challenge.* AAHE-ERIC Higher Education Research Report No. 4. Washington, D.C.: American Association for Higher Education. ED 144 439. 102 pp. MF–01; PC–05.

Lawrence, Janet H., and Robert T. Blackburn. 1988. "Age as a Predictor of Faculty Productivity: Three Conceptual Approaches." *Journal of Higher Education* 59(1): 22–38.

Layzell, Daniel T., and Jan W. Lyddon. 1990. *Budgeting for Higher Education at the State Level: Enigma, Paradox, and Ritual.* ASHE-ERIC Higher Education Report No. 4. Washington, D.C.: George Washington Univ., School of Education and Human Development. ED 327 130. 134 pp. MF–01; PC–06.

Levin, Henry M. 1991. "Raising Productivity in Higher Education." *Journal of Higher Education* 62(3): 241–62.

Levine, Arthur, and Ernest Boyer. 1981. *A Quest for Common Learning: The Aims of General Education.* Princeton, N.J.: Carnegie Foundation for the Advancement of Teaching. ED 200 298. 77 pp. MF–01; PC not available EDRS.

Leviton, L., and E. Hughes. 1981. "Research on the Utilization of Evaluations: A Review and Synthesis." *Evaluation Review* 5(4): 525–48.

Light, R.J. 1990. *The Harvard Assessment Seminars: Explorations with Students and Faculty about Teaching, Learning, and Student Life.* First Report. Cambridge, Mass.: Harvard Graduate School of Education and Kennedy School of Government.

Likins, Peter. 9 May 1990. "In an Era of Tight Budgets and Public Criticism, Colleges Must Rethink Their Goals and Priorities." *Chronicle of Higher Education* 36: B1–B2.

Lindsay, A.W. 1992. "Concepts of Quality in Higher Education." *Journal of Tertiary Education Administration* 14(2): 153–63.

———. 1993. "Performance and Quality in Higher Education." *Australian Universities' Review* 36(1): 32–35.

———. 1994. "Quality and Management in Universities." *Journal of Tertiary Education Administration* 16(1): 55–68.

Linke, Russell D. 1990. "Australia." In *The Development of Performance Indicators for Higher Education: A Compendium for Eleven Countries,* edited by H.R. Kells. Paris: Organization for Economic Cooperation and Development. ED 331 355. 134 pp. MF–01; PC not available EDRS.

———. 1992. "Some Principles for Application of Performance Indicators in Higher Education." *Higher Education Management* 4(2): 194–203.

Lively, Kit. 2 September 1992. " 'Accountability' of Colleges Gets Renewed Scrutiny from State Officials." *Chronicle of Higher Education* 49(2): A25–26.

———. 2 March 1994. "Incentive Financing for Colorado's Colleges." *Chronicle of Higher Education:* A22.

Lonsdale, A. 1993. "Changes in Incentives, Rewards, and Sanctions." *Higher Education Management* 5(2): 223–36.

Lucier, P. 1992. "Performance Indicators in Higher Education: Lowering the Tension of the Debate." *Higher Education Management* 4(2): 204–14.

Maassen, R., and F. van Vught. 1988. "An Intriguing Janus Head: The Two Faces of the New Governmental Strategy for Higher Education in the Netherlands." *European Journal of Education* 23(1/2): 65–76.

McClain, C. 1992. "Draft Clarifying Comments and Definitions for the Goals Recommended by the CBHE Task Force on Critical Choices for Higher Education." A letter to the presidents and chancellors of Missouri public and independent colleges and universities. Jefferson City: Missouri Coordinating Board for Higher Education.

McElwee, G. 1992. "How Useful Are Performance Indicators in the Polytechnic Sector?" *Educational Management and Administration* 20(3): 189–92.

McKeachie, W.J. 1980. "Class Size, Large Classes, and Multiple Sections." *Academe* 66: 24–27.

McKeachie, W.J., P.R. Pintrich, G. Lin, and D. Smith. 1987. *Teaching and Learning in the College Classroom: A Review of the Research Literature.* Ann Arbor: Univ. of Michigan, National Center for Research to Improve Teaching and Learning. ED 314 999. 124 pp. MF–01; PC–05.

McKenna, Joseph F. 4 November 1991. "TQ Government." *Industry Week* 240: 12–18.

———. 21 June 1993. "Total Quality Government: More Than Political Fashion." *Industry Week* 242(12): 44–46.

McKeown, Mary P. Summer 1989. "State Funding Formulas for Public Institutions of Higher Education." *Journal of Education Finance* 15: 101–12.

Maclean's. 1992. "Special Report. Measuring Excellence" 105(4): 20–36.

McMahon, Eleanor M. 1986. "The Why, What, and Who of Assessment: The State Perspective." Denver: Education Commission of the States. ED 284 892. 13 pp. MF–01; PC–01.

McNeil, D.R. 7 June 1989 "Technology Is a Hot Topic, but Its Impact on Higher Education Has Been Minimal." *Chronicle of Higher Education* 35(39): A44.

McVicar, M. 1990. "Quality Assessment in British Higher Education."

In *Peer Review and Performance Indicators: Quality Assessment in British and Dutch Higher Education,* edited by L. Goedege-buure, P. Maassen, and D. Westerheijden. Utrecht: Uitgeverij Lemma B.V.

Maeroff, Gene I. 15 October 1993. "Teaching: The Facts, as I See Them." *Wall Street Journal.* Letters to the Editor.

Magner, Denise K. 26 January 1994. "Association of University Pro-fessors Challenges the Belief that Professors Are Underworked." *Chronicle of Higher Education:* A18.

Marchese, Ted J. 1985. "Let's Reward Quality: Tennessee's Bold Exper-iment." *Change* 17(6): 37–45.

———. 1987. "Third Down, Ten Years to Go." *AAHE Bulletin* 40(4): 3–8.

———. May 1994. "What Is the Status of Assessment Today? A Key-note Address." In *Faculty Perspectives: Sharing Ideas on Assess-ment.* Albany: SUNY Faculty Senate.

Marcus, Jon. 22 September 1993. "College Costs Exceed Income, Inflation: Despite Slashed Services, Average Fees Jump in All Cate-gories." *Houston Chronicle.*

Martin, L.M. 1994. *Equity and General Performance Indicators in Higher Education.* Vol. 1/2. Equity Indicators. Canberra: Australian Government Publishing Service.

Massy, William F. 1991. "Improving Productivity in Higher Education: Administration and Support Costs." Stanford, Calif.: Forum for Col-lege Financing. ED 333 813. 13 pp. MF–01; PC–01.

Massy, William F., and Joel Meyerson. 1992. *Strategy and Finance in Higher Education: Surviving the '90s.* Princeton, N.J.: Peterson's Guides.

———, eds. 1994. *Measuring Institutional Performance in Higher Education.* Stanford Forum for Higher Education Futures. Prince-ton, N.J.: Peterson's Guides.

Massy, William F., and A. Wilger. 1992. "Productivity in Postsecondary Education: A New Approach." *Educational Evaluation and Policy Analysis* 14(4): 361–76.

Massy, William F., and Robert Zemsky. 1990. "The Dynamics of Aca-demic Productivity: A Seminar." Denver: State Higher Education Executive Officers. ED 327 079. 47 pp. MF–01; PC–02.

———. 1992. "Faculty Discretionary Time: Departments and the Academic Ratchet." *Policy Perspectives* 4(3): 3B–4B.

Meisinger, Richard, Jr., and Leroy Dubeck. 1984. *College and Uni-versity Budgeting: An Introduction for Faculty and Academic Administrators.* Washington, D.C.: National Association of College and University Business Officers. ED 257 348. 336 pp. MF–01; PC not available EDRS.

Mentkowski, M., and G.P. Rogers. 1988. *Establishing the Validity of Measures of College Student Outcomes.* Milwaukee: Alverno College, Office of Research and Evaluation.

Mertens, F., and R. Bormans. 1990. "Background to the Development of a System of Performance Indicators in the Netherlands." In *Management Information and Performance Indicators in Higher Education: An International Issue,* edited by F. Dochy et. al. Assen, the Netherlands: Van Gorcum & Co.

Middaugh, Michael F., and David E. Hollowell. 1992. "Examining Academic and Administrative Productivity Measures." In *Containing Costs and Improving Productivity in Higher Education,* edited by C.S. Hollins. New Directions for Institutional Research No. 75. San Francisco: Jossey-Bass.

Mikesell, John L. 1982. *Fiscal Administration: Analysis of Applications for the Public Sector.* Homewood, Ill.: Dorsey Press.

Mingle, James R. May 1989. "The Political Meaning of Quality." *AAHE Bulletin:* 8–11. ED 308 748. 4 pp. MF–01; PC–01.

Minter, John. 1992. "Trends in E&G Expenditure Allocations: Indicators of Recession or Increased Productivity?" *NACUBO Business Officer* 26(2): 26–31.

Morgan, Anthony W. 1990. "State-Level Quality Incentives: A Mosaic of Political, Managerial, and Technical Complexity." In *Developing State Fiscal Incentives to Improve Higher Education.* College Park, Md.: National Center for Postsecondary Governance and Finance.

———. 1992. "The Politics and Policies of Selective Funding: The Case of State-Level Quality Incentives." *Review of Higher Education* 15(3): 289–306.

Moses, I. 1990. "Teaching, Research, and Scholarship in Different Disciplines." *Higher Education* 19(3): 351–75.

Moss, Charles, and Gerald Gaither. 1976. "Formula Budgeting: Requiem or Renaissance?" *Journal of Higher Education* 47: 543–63.

Muffo, John. 1993. "Assessment in Great Britain: An Alternative View." *Assessment Update* 5(1): 9+.

Murray, Charles, and R.J. Herrnstein. Winter 1992. "What's Really behind the SAT Score Decline?" *Public Interest* 106: 32–56.

Nadeau, Gilles G. 1992. "The Use of Quality and Excellence Indicators in Postsecondary Education." *CSSHE Professional File* 10: 1–17. ED 354 824. 17 pp. MF–01; PC–01.

National Center for Education Statistics. 1991. *Education Counts: An Indicator System to Monitor the Nation's Educational Health.* Washington, D.C.: U.S. Government Printing Office. ED 334 279. 121 pp. MF–01; PC–05.

———. 1994a. *Education in States and Nations.* Washington, D.C.: U.S. Government Printing Office.

———. 1994b. *A Preliminary Study of the Feasibility and Utility for National Policy on Instructional "Good Practice" Indicators in Undergraduate Education.* Washington, D.C.: U.S. Dept. of Education. ED 372 718. 68 pp. MF–01; PC–03.

National Center for Higher Education Management Systems. 1992. *An Evaluation of the Ohio Selective Excellence Program: Displays for Background Data Analysis.* Report submitted to the Legislative Oversight Bureau, the Management and Budget Office, and the Ohio Board of Regents. Boulder, Colo.: Author.

———. February 1993a. *NCHEMS News 6.*

———. 1993b. "A Preliminary Study of the Feasibility and Utility for National Policy on Instructional 'Good Practice' Indicators in Undergraduate Education." Prepared for the National Center for Education Statistics. Boulder, Colo.: Author.

National Education Goals Panel. 1993a. *National Education Goals Report. Vol. 1—The National Report.* Washington, D.C. Author.

———. 1993b. *National Education Goals Report. Vol. 2—State Reports.* Washington, D.C.: Author.

Neal, John E. 1990. "An Examination of Disciplinary Differences in Factors Related to Job Satisfaction among Liberal Arts College Faculty Members." Paper presented at a meeting of the Association for the Study of Higher Education, November, Portland, Oregon. ED 326 124. 49 pp. MF–01; PC–02.

Nedwek, Brian P. 1992. "Remarks at the President's Conference on Outcomes Assessment and Institutional Effectiveness." St. Louis: St. Louis Univ.

———. 1993. "Self-Study Project Management Strategies: Turning Institutional Assessment into Actionable Outcomes." *A Collection of Papers on Self-Study and Institutional Improvement.* Chicago: North Central Association of Colleges and Schools.

———. 1994. "The Leap of Faith in Institutional Effectiveness Assessment: Rediscovering Process." *A Collection of Papers on Self-Study and Institutional Improvement.* Chicago: North Central Association of Colleges and Schools. ED 370 503. 275 pp. MF–01; PC–11.

Nedwek, Brian P., and John E. Neal. 1994a. "Informational Cultures: Facing Challenges of Institutional Research within Cross-Continental Settings." *Research in Higher Education* 35(4): 429–42.

———. 1994b. "Performance Indicators and Rational Management Tools: A Comparative Assessment of Projects in North America and Europe." *Research in Higher Education* 35(1): 75–103.

Newman, Frank. 1985. "Rising Expectations: Can States Help Renew Quality?" *Change* 17(6): 12–15.

———. 1987. *Choosing Quality: Reducing Conflict between the State and the University.* Denver: Education Commission of the States. ED 305 848. 135 pp. MF–01; PC–06.

Newsom, W., and C. Hayes. 1990. "Are Mission Statements Worthwhile?" *Planning for Higher Education* 19: 28–30.

Newton, R. 1992. "The Two Cultures of Academe: An Overlooked Planning Hurdle." *Planning for Higher Education* 21: 8–14.

Nichols, James O. 1991a. *The Departmental Guide to Implementation of Student Outcomes Assessment and Institutional Effectiveness.* New York: Agathon Press.

————. 1991b. *A Practitioner's Handbook for Institutional Effectiveness and Student Outcomes Assessment Implementation.* New York: Agathon Press.

Niiniluoto, I. 1990. "Finland." In *The Development of Performance Indicators for Higher Education: A Compendium for Eleven Countries,* edited by H.R. Kells. Paris: Organization for Economic Cooperation and Development. ED 331 355. 134 pp. MF–01; PC not available EDRS.

Noble, John H., Jr., Arthur G. Cryns, and Bertha S. Laury. 1992. "Faculty Productivity and Costs: A Multivariate Analysis." *Evaluation Review* 16(3): 288–314.

Noe, Roger C. 1986. "Formula Funding in Higher Education: A Review." *Journal of Education Finance* 11: 363–76.

North Central Association. 1993. *Handbook of Accreditation: 1993–94.* Working draft. Chicago: Commission on Institutions of Higher Education.

O'Neil, R.M. 1994. "Quality and Higher Education: Australia and the United States." *Journal of Tertiary Education Administration* 16(1): 135–40.

Organization for Economic Cooperation and Development. 1987. *Universities under Scrutiny.* Paris: Author. ED 283 449. 117 pp. MF–01; PC not available EDRS.

————. 1988. *Performance Indicators in Higher Education: A Study of Their Development and Use in 15 OECD Countries.* Paris: Author.

Osborne, David, and Ted Gaebler. 1993. *Reinventing Government: How the Entrepreneurial Spirit Is Transforming the Public Sector.* New York: Penguin Books, Plume Book.

Ouchi, W. 1989. "Markets, Bureaucracies, and Clans." *Administrative Science Quarterly* 25(1): 129–41.

Paardekooper, C.M., and A. Spee. 1990. "A Government Perspective on Quality Assessment in Dutch Higher Education." In *Peer Review and Performance Indicators: Quality Assessment in British and Dutch Higher Education,* edited by L. Goedegebuure, P. Maassen, and D. Westerheijden. Utrecht: Uitgeverij Lemma B.V.

Pascarella, E.T., and P.T. Terenzini. 1991. *How College Affects Students: Findings and Insights from Twenty Years of Research.* San Francisco: Jossey-Bass.

Paulson, Christine P. 1990. *State Initiatives in Assessment and Outcome Measurement: Tools for Teaching and Learning in the 1990s.* Denver: Education Commission of the States. ED 321 701. 115 pp. MF–01; PC–05.

Penrod, J.I., and M.G. Dolence. 1992. *Reengineering: A Process for*

Transforming Higher Education. Professional Paper Series No. 9. Boulder, Colo.: Association for the Management of Information Technology in Higher Education. ED 345 651. 44 pp. MF–01; PC–02.

Peters, M. 1992. "Performance Indicators in New Zealand Higher Education: Accountability or Control?" *Journal of Education Policy* 7(3): 267–83.

Peterson, M., and M. Spencer. 1993. "Qualitative and Quantitative Approaches to Academic Culture: Do They Tell Us the Same Thing?" In *Higher Education: Handbook of Theory and Research*, edited by John C. Smart. Vol. 9. New York: Agathon Press.

Peterson's, Inc., and Association of Governing Boards. 1992. *Survey of Strategic Indicators*. Princeton, N.J.: Peterson's, Inc.

Pollitt, C. 1989. "Performance Indicators in the Longer Term." *Public Money and Management* 9(3): 51–55.

Polytechnics and Colleges Funding Council. 1992. *Macro Performance Indicators*. Bristol, Eng.: Author.

Porter, Michael E. 1990. *The Competitive Advantage of Nations*. New York: Free Press.

Posner, Bruce G., and Lawrence R. Rothstein. 1994. "Reinventing the Business of Government: An Interview with Change Catalyst David Osborne." *Harvard Business Review* 72(3): 132–43.

Ratcliff, J.L., ed. 1992. "Assessment and Curriculum Reform." In *New Directions for Higher Education No. 80*. San Francisco: Jossey-Bass.

Richardson, R.C., Jr. 1994a. "Effectiveness in Undergraduate Education: An Analysis of State Quality Indicators." In *Charting Higher Education Accountability: A Sourcebook on State-Level Performance Indicators,* edited by Sandra S. Ruppert. Denver: Education Commission of the States. ED 375 789. 177 pp. MF–01; PC–08.

———. 1994b. "Effectiveness in Undergraduate Education: An Analysis of State Quality Indicators." ECS Working Papers (Draft). Denver: Education Commission of the States.

———. 1994c. "Illinois." In *Charting Higher Education Accountability: A Sourcebook on State-Level Performance Indicators,* edited by Sandra S. Ruppert. Denver: Education Commission of the States. ED 375 789. 177 pp. MF–01; PC–08.

———. 1994d. "Illinois." ECS Working Papers (Draft). Denver: Education Commission of the States.

———. 1994e. "Indicators of Quality in Undergraduate Education." ECS Working Papers (Draft). Denver: Education Commission of the States.

———. 1994f. "The State University of New York." In *Charting Higher Education Accountability: A Sourcebook on State-Level Performance Indicators,* edited by Sandra S. Ruppert. Denver: Education Commission of the States. ED 375 789. 177 pp. MF–01; PC–08.

———. 1994g. "The State University of New York." ECS Working Papers (Draft). Denver: Education Commission of the States.

Rockart, J.F., and J.E. Short. 1990. "The Networked Organization and the Management of Interdependence." In *The Corporation of the 1990s: Information and Organizational Transformation,* edited by T.J. Allen and M.S. Scott Morton. New York: Oxford Univ. Press.

Rossi, P. 1978. "Issues in the Evaluation of Human Services Delivery." *Evaluation Quarterly* 2: 573–99.

Rossi, P., and H. Freeman. 1989. *Evaluation: A Systematic Approach.* 4th ed. Newbury Park, Calif.: Sage Publications.

Rudolph, Frederick. 1984. "The Power of Professors: The Impact of Specialization and Professionalization on the Curriculum." *Change* 16(4): 12–17.

Rullmann, P.M.M. 1990. "A Nonuniversity Perspective on Quality Assessment in the Netherlands." In *Peer Review and Performance Indicators: Quality Assessment in British and Dutch Higher Education,* edited by L. Goedegebuure, P. Maassen, and D. Westerheijden. Utrecht: Uitgeverij Lemma B.V.

Ruppert, Sandra S. 1994a. "Kentucky." In *Charting Higher Education Accountability: A Sourcebook on State-Level Performance Indicators,* edited by Sandra S. Ruppert. Denver: Education Commission of the States. ED 375 789. 177 pp. MF–01; PC–08.

———. 1994b. "Kentucky." ECS Working Papers (Draft). Denver: Education Commission of the States.

———. 1994c. "South Carolina." In *Charting Higher Education Accountability: A Sourcebook on State-Level Performance Indicators,* edited by Sandra S. Ruppert. Denver: Education Commission of the States. ED 375 789. 177 pp. MF–01; PC–08.

———. 1994d. "South Carolina." ECS Working Papers (Draft). Denver: Education Commission of the States.

———, ed. 1994e. *Charting Higher Education Accountability: A Sourcebook on State-Level Performance Indicators.* Denver: Education Commission of the States. ED 375 789. 177 pp. MF–01; PC–08.

Rush, S.C. 1992. "Productivity or Quality?" In *Productivity and Higher Education,* edited by R.E. Anderson and J.W. Meyerson. Princeton, N.J.: Peterson's Guides.

———. 1994. "Benchmarking: How Good Is Good?" In *Measuring Institutional Performance in Higher Education,* edited by W.F. Massy and J.W. Meyerson. Princeton, N.J.: Peterson's Guides.

Russell, Alene Bycer. 1992. *Faculty Workload: State and System Perspectives.* Denver: State Higher Education Executive Officers/Education Commission of the States. ED 356 728. 78 pp. MF–01; PC–04.

Rutherford, Desmond. 1987. "Indicators of Performance: Some Practical Suggestions." *Assessment and Evaluation in Higher Education* 12(1): 46–55.

Sander, G.F. 26 May 1993. "Dutch Lawmakers Give Universities Autonomy in Exchange for Greater Quality Control." *Chronicle of Higher Education:* A35–A36.

―――. 14 December 1994a. "New Minister Would Undo Some Reforms at Sweden's Universities." *Chronicle of Higher Education:* A43.

―――. 20 April 1994b. "Wave of Reform Crests in Denmark." *Chronicle of Higher Education:* A47–A49.

Sapp, M.M. 1993. "Setting Up a Key Success Indices Report: A How-to Manual." Paper presented at the 33rd Annual Forum of the Association for Institutional Research, May 17, Chicago, Illinois. ED 360 909. 26 pp. MF–01; PC–02.

Sapp, M.M., and M.L. Temares. 1991. "Being Competitive in Time: Key Success Indices." Paper presented at the 31st Annual Forum of the Association for Institution Research, May 27, San Francisco, California. ED 336 016. 24 pp. MF–01; PC–01.

―――. 1992. "A Monthly Checkup: Key Success Indices Track Health of the University of Miami." *NACUBO Business Officer* 25(9): 24–31.

Schilling, K., and K. Schilling. 1993. "Descriptive Approaches to Assessment: Moving beyond Meeting Requirements to Making a Difference." In *A Collection of Papers on Self-Study and Institutional Improvements.* Chicago: North Central Association of Colleges and Schools. ED 356 712. 214 pp. MF–01; PC–09.

Schmidtlein, Frank A. 1989–90. "Why Linking Budgets to Plans Has Proven Difficult in Higher Education." *Planning for Higher Education* 18(2): 9–23.

―――. 1990. "Planning for Quality: Perils and Possibilities." Paper presented at an annual forum of the European Association for Institutional Research. ED 328 188. 20 pp. MF–01; PC–01.

Schmitz, C.C. 1993. "Assessing the Validity of Higher Education Indicators." *Journal of Higher Education* 64(5): 503–21.

Schoor, Juliet. 1991. *The Overworked American: The Unexpected Decline of Leisure.* New York: Basic Books.

Scottish Centrally Funded Colleges. June 1992. *Performance Indicators.* Report of proceedings of a seminar held in September 1991 at Glasgow Polytechnic.

Scottish Higher Education Funding Council. October 1992. "Quality Framework." Glasgow: Author.

Segers, M., W. Wijnen, and F. Dochy. 1990. "Performance Indicators: A New Management Tool for Higher Education? The Case of the United Kingdom, the Netherlands, and Australia." In *Management Information and Performance Indicators in Higher Education: An International Issue,* edited by F. Dochy, M. Segers, and W. Wijnen. Assen, the Netherlands: Van Gorcum & Co.

Seymour, Daniel J. 1993. *On Q: Causing Quality in Higher Education.* Oryx Series on Higher Education. Washington, D.C.: American Council on Education.

Sharp, John. 1993. *Against the Grain: High-Quality, Low-Cost Government in Texas.* Vol. 1/2. A Report from the Texas Performance

Review. Austin: Office of the Texas Comptroller of Public Accounts.

Sherr, Lawrence, and Deborah Teeter, eds. 1991. *Total Quality Management in Higher Education.* New Directions for Institutional Research No. 71. San Francisco: Jossey-Bass.

Sims, Serbrenia J. 1992. *Student Outcomes Assessment: A Historical Review and Guide to Program Development.* Contributions to the Study of Education No. 52. Westport, Conn.: Greenwood Press.

Sizer, John. 1989. "Performance Indicators and Quality Control in Higher Education." Keynote address to the International Conference of the Institute of Education. London, England.

———. 1990a. "Funding Councils and Performance Indicators in Quality Assessment in the United Kingdom." In *Peer Review and Performance Indicators: Quality Assessment in British and Dutch Higher Education,* edited by L. Goedegebuure, P. Maassen, and D. Westerheijden. Utrecht: Uitgeverij Lemma B.V.

———. 1990b. "Performance Indicators and the Management of Universities in the U.K.: A Summary of Developments with Commentary." In *Management Information and Performance Indicators in Higher Education: An International Issue,* edited by F. Dochy, M. Segers, and W. Wijnen. Assen, the Netherlands: Van Gorcum & Co.

———. 1992. "Performance Indicators in Government–Higher Education Institutions Relationships: Lessons for Government." *Higher Education Management* 4(2): 156–63.

Sizer, J., A. Spee, and R. Bormans. 1992. "The Role of Performance Indicators in Higher Education." *Higher Education* 24(2): 133–56.

Slaughter, Sheila. 1985. "From Serving Students to Serving the Economy: Changing Expectations of Faculty Role Performance." *Higher Education* 14: 41–56.

Smartt, Steven. 1984. "Linking Program Reviews to the Budget." In *Financial Incentives for Academic Quality,* edited by John Folger. New Directions for Higher Education No. 48. San Francisco: Jossey-Bass.

Smith, D.C. September 1992. "Meeting the Challenges." Discussion paper based on the work of the Principals Advisory Task Force on Resource Issues. Kingston, Ontario: Queen's Univ.

Smith, S.L. 1991. *Report of the Commission of Inquiry on Canadian University Education.* Ottawa: Association of Universities and Colleges of Canada.

Smith, V. 1993. "Phantom Students: Student Mobility and General Education." *AAHE Newsletter* 45(10): 10–13+.

Snowdon, K. 1993. "The Development of Performance Indicators at Queen's University." Paper presented at a conference of Canadian Institutional Researchers and Planners, Vancouver, British Columbia.

Southern Association of Colleges and Schools. 1989. *Resource Man-*

ual on Institutional Effectiveness. 2d ed. Atlanta: Commission on Colleges.

Spee, A., and R. Bormans. 1992. "Performance Indicators in Government-Institutional Relations: The Conceptual Framework." *Higher Education Management* 4(2): 139–55.

State University of New York. September 1992. *Assessment at SUNY: Principles, Processes, and Case Studies.* Albany: SUNY, University Faculty Senate.

———. Spring 1993. *Quality Academics, Quality Productivity.* Albany: Author.

———. May 1994. *Faculty Perspectives: Sharing Ideas on Assessment.* Albany: SUNY, University Faculty Senate.

Stecklow, Steve. 28 February 1994. "More Colleges Offer Degrees in Three Years." *Wall Street Journal* (eastern edition).

Steers, R., and L. Porter. 1983. *Motivation and Work Behavior.* 3d ed. New York: McGraw-Hill.

Stolte-Heiskanen, V. 1992. "Research Performance Evaluation in the Higher Education Sector: A Grass-Roots Perspective." *Higher Education Management* 4(2): 179–93.

"Strengthening Accountability in Wisconsin." 1994. *NASULGC Newsline* 3(2): 3.

Sykes, Charles J. 1988. *ProfScam: Professors and the Demise of Higher Education.* Washington, D.C.: Regnery Gateway.

Taylor, B.E., J.W. Meyerson, and W. Massy. 1993. *Strategic Indicators for Higher Education: Improving Performance.* Princeton, N.J.: Peterson's Guides.

Taylor, B.E., J.W. Meyerson, L.R. Morrell, and D.G. Park, Jr. 1991. *Strategic Analysis: Using Comparative Data to Understand Your Institution.* Washington, D.C.: Association of Governing Boards of Universities and Colleges.

Taylor, J. 1987. "Performance Indicators in Higher Education: Recent Developments in U.K. Universities." *Australian Universities' Review* 30(2): 28–31.

Teather, D. 1990a. "Performance Indicators in Australian Higher Education: The Context and an Appraisal of the 1988 Report." In *Management Information and Performance Indicators in Higher Education: An International Issue,* edited by F. Dochy, M. Segers, and W. Wijnen. Assen, the Netherlands: Van Gorcum & Co.

Teather, D. 1990b. "Report of the Australian AVCC/ACDP Working Party on Performance Indicators." In *Management Information and Performance Indicators in Higher Education: An International Issue,* edited by F. Dochy, M. Segers, and W. Wijnen. Assen, the Netherlands: Van Gorcum & Co.

Teeter, Deborah, and G. Gregory Lozier, eds. 1993. *Pursuit of Quality in Higher Education: Case Studies in Total Quality Management.* New Directions for Institutional Research No. 78. San Francisco:

Jossey-Bass.

Temple, P., and D. Whitechurch. 1994. "The New Entrepreneurship in British Higher Education." *Planning for Higher Education* 22(3): 13–18.

Terenzini, P.T. 1993. "Cross-National Themes in the Assessment of Quality in Higher Education." *Assessment Update* 5(3): 1–3.

Thurow, Lester C. 1993. *Head to Head: The Coming Economic Battle among Japan, Europe, and America*. New York: Warner Books.

Tomlinson, Tommy M. 1988. *Class Size and Public Policy: Politics and Panaceas*. Washington, D.C.: U.S. Dept. of Education, Office of Educational Research and Improvement. ED 292 216. 49 pp. MF–01; PC–02.

Toombs, William, and William G. Tierney. 1991. *Meeting the Mandate: Renewing the College and Departmental Curriculum*. ASHE-ERIC Higher Education Report No. 6. Washington, D.C.: George Washington Univ., School of Education and Human Development. ED 345 603. 124 pp. MF–01; PC–05.

Torrance, H. 1993. "Combining Measurement-Driven Instruction with Authentic Assessment: Some Initial Observations of National Assessment in England and Wales." *Educational Evaluation and Policy Analysis* 15(1): 81–90.

Townsend, B., L. Newell, and M. Wiese. 1992. *Creating Distinctiveness: Lessons from Uncommon Colleges and Universities*. ASHE-ERIC Higher Education Report No. 6. Washington, D.C.: George Washington Univ., School of Education and Human Development. ED 356 702. 110 pp. MF–01; PC–05.

Turk, F.J. July 1992. "The ABC's of Activity-Based Costing." *NACUBO Business Officer* 26(1): 36–43.

U.S. Department of Education. 1983. *A Nation at Risk: The Imperative for Educational Reform*. Washington, D.C.: National Commission on Excellence in Education.

———. 1991. *America 2000: An Education Strategy*. Washington, D.C.: U.S. Government Printing Office.

———. 1992. *National Assessment of College Student Learning: Issues and Concerns*. Washington, D.C.: Office of Educational Research and Improvement. ED 346 808. 118 pp. MF–01; PC–05.

Universities Funding Council. 1992. "Research Assessment Exercise 1992." Circular Letter 5/92. Bristol, Eng.: Author.

"Universities Grapple with Productivity: Legislators Demanding More Bang for the Tax Buck." 1994. *NASULGC Newsline* 3(2): 1–3.

University of Wisconsin System. 1994. *Accountability for Achievement: 1994 Report on Accountability Indicators*. Madison: Author.

U.S. News and World Report. 28 September 1992. "America's Best Colleges 1993": 96–98+.

Van de Water, Gordon B. 1994a. "Colorado." In *Charting Higher Education Accountability: A Sourcebook on State-Level Performance*

Indicators, edited by Sandra S. Ruppert. Denver: Education Commission of the States. ED 375 789. 177 pp. MF–01; PC–08.

———. 1994b. "Florida." In *Charting Higher Education Accountability: A Sourcebook on State-Level Performance Indicators,* edited by Sandra S. Ruppert. Denver: Education Commission of the States. ED 375 789. 177 pp. MF–01; PC–08.

———. 1994c. "Florida." ECS Working Papers (Draft). Denver: Education Commission of the States.

van Vught, F.A. 1988. "A New Autonomy in European Higher Education? An Explanation and Analysis of the Strategy of Self-Regulation in Higher Education." *International Journal of Institutional Management in Higher Education* 12: 16–26.

van Vught, F.A., and D.F. Westerheijden. 1992. *Quality Management and Quality Assurance in European Higher Education.* Enschede, the Netherlands: Center for Higher Education Policy Studies.

———. 1993. *Quality Management and Quality Assurance in European Higher Education: Methods and Mechanisms.* Luxembourg: Office for Official Publications of the EC.

Von Linstow, H. 1990. "Denmark." In *The Development of Performance Indicators for Higher Education: A Compendium for Eleven Countries,* edited by H.R. Kells. Paris: Organization for Economic Cooperation and Development. ED 331 355. 134 pp. MF–01; PC not available EDRS.

Vroeijenstijn, T.I, and H. Acherman. 1990. "Control-Oriented versus Improvement-Oriented Quality Assessment." In *Peer Review and Performance Indicators: Quality Assessment in British and Dutch Higher Education,* edited by L. Goedegebuure, P. Maassen, and D. Westerheijden. Utrecht: Uitgeverij Lemma B.V.

Webster, D. 1992. "Rankings of Undergraduate Education in *U.S. News & World Report* and *Money:* Are They Any Good?" *Change* 24(2): 19–31.

Weiss, C. 1977. *Using Social Research in Public Policy Making.* Lexington, Mass.: Lexington Books.

West, Peter. 1988. "Performance Indicators in U.K. Universities: The Example of the University of Strathclyde." *International Journal of Institutional Management in Higher Education* 12(2): 218–21.

Westerheijden, D.F. 1990. "Peers, Performance, and Power: Quality Assessment in the Netherlands." In *Peer Review and Performance Indicators: Quality Assessment in British and Dutch Higher Education,* edited by L. Goedegebuure, P. Maassen, and D. Westerheijden. Utrecht: Uitgeverij Lemma B.V.

Whitaker's Almanac. 1994. London: J. Whitaker & Sons.

Wilcox, B. 1990. "Is There a Role for Site Visits in Monitoring Systems? A U.K. Perspective." *Evaluation and Research in Education* 4(2): 81–91.

Williams, D., P. Cook, B. Quinn, and R. Jensen. 1985. "University Class

Size: Is Smaller Better?" *Research in Higher Education* 23(3): 307–18.

Williams, G. 1990. "The Financial Revolution at British Universities." *Planning for Higher Education* 19(1): 27–30.

Winona State University. 1994a. "Long-Range Plan." Winona, Minn.: Author.

———. 1994b. "Mission and Goals, Quality Assurance, and Assessment Plan." Winona, Minn.: Author.

Yorke, M. 1991a. *Performance Indicators: Observations on Their Use in the Assurance of Course Quality.* CNAA Project Report 30. London: Council for National Academic Awards.

———. 1991b. "Performance Indicators: Towards a Synoptic Framework." *Higher Education* 21(2): 235–48.

———. 1993. "Performance Indicators and the Enhancement of Programme Quality." Paper presented at the 33rd Annual Forum of the Association for Institutional Research, May 17, Chicago, Illinois.

Young, D. 1990. "The Academic Audit Unit: An Organization for University Quality Assessment." In *Peer Review and Performance Indicators: Quality Assessment in British and Dutch Higher Education,* edited by L. Goedegebuure, P. Maassen, and D. Westerheijden. Utrecht: Uitgeverij Lemma B.V.

Zemsky, R., and W.F. Massy. November/December 1990. "Cost Containment: Committing to a New Economic Reality." *Change* 22: 16–22.

INDEX

A

Academic Audit Unit. See Quality Audit group

Accountability Task Force, 34

accountability imperative, 1

Accreditation agencies, viewing with suspicion, 38

ACT scores, ix

administrative rather than professional accountability, reliance on, 85

AGB. See Association of Governing Boards of Universities and Colleges

Alberta, planning indicators of, 61

American Council on Education, 1

"An Open Market for Higher Education," 78

approaches to quality measurement in Canada, 61

Arkansas, development of productivity goals by, 2

Association of College Directors and Principals, 5

Association of Cooperating Universities, 69, 70

Association of Governing Boards of Universities and Colleges, 28, 38

     biennial survey of strategic indicators, 91

Australia, 4

     demanded more educational response to government priorities, 6

     reason for performance indicator development, 5

     use of performance indicators, 62-68

Australian Catholic University, 63

Australian Vice Chancellors Committee, 5

autonomy increase combined with stringent standards of quality, 68

B

binary educational system, final abolition of, 52, 53

block grants as part of special-purpose budget, 40

Bovey Commission, 60

British Columbia, planning indicators of, 61

British, use different terminology with same meaning for indicators, 44

bureaucracies as locus of control for performance indicators, 49

Burke, Provost Joseph, 6

C

Canada effort, 60

Canada, use of performance indicators, 59-62

capital budget, 39

Carnegie Foundation for the Advancement of Teaching, 14

clans as locus of control for performance indicators, 49

Colorado

     adoption of form of incentive funding by, 2

Fund for the Improvement of Post Secondary Education, xiii, 31
funding for results, 2
Further and Higher Education Act of 1992, 53, 54
future of academy, recent trends that will help shape, 84

G

Georgia, provided significant independence to higher education
    system, 37
goal-oriented performance, notion of excellence based on, 2
Goals 2000: Educate America Act, 37
goals and expectations, general areas of developing interest, 42
goals of creativity, initiative, and learning, 24
"good practice indicators," development of, 28, 30, 31
government review of evidence of quality, federal, 11
graduate level education, U.S. performance indicators don't
    recognize, 45
Great Britain. See United Kingdom

H

HESA. See Higher Education Statistics Agency
Higher Education and Research Act, 69, 70
Higher Education Council in Australia, 66
Higher Education Development Act of 1987, 73
Higher Education Quality Council, 54, 58
Higher Education Statistics Agency, 54
Higher Education: A New Framework, 53
Higher Education: A Policy Statement, 64

I

Illinois, state included in ECS project, 31
impact on students' learning, need to measure, 51
incentive funding, 2, 41
        demise of, 4
indicator survey of colleges and universities, 28
indicators of social equity, 64
initiative (competitive) funding as part of special-purpose
    budget, 40-41
institutional context indicators, 64
institutional effectiveness, 13
institutional efficiency, 13
internal indicators, 64
International Indicator Systems, comparison of, 79-80

J

Joint Performance Indicators Working Group, 59

K

K-12 connection, 36

Kentucky
   emulated South Carolina's report card bill, 7
   linking accountability reform from kindergarten to
      college, 36
   of value of lower student/faculty ratios, 7
   state included in ECS project, 31

L

legislation by fax, 33
lower student/faculty ratio assumed associated with greater cognitive
   gain, 7

M

Malcolm Baldrige National Quality Award, 11
management by instruction change to management by
   objectives, 75
"management technology," 57
market driven, higher education will remain driven by, 84
markets as locus of control for performance indicators, 49
mechanistic view of education, 55
Middle States Association accreditation agency, 38
Missouri
   "Funding for Results" program of, 41
   performance funding by, 2, 41

N

NACUBO. See National Association of College and University Business Officers
National Association of College and University Business Officers,
   26, 27
National Benchmarking Project
   attempt to apply multiple performance indicators, 91
   functional areas in, 27
National Board of Employment, Education, and Training, 66
National Center for Education Statistics, 23, 89
   collecting and publishing indicators, 26
National Center for Higher Education Management Systems,
   28, 30-31, 83-84
National Council of Teachers of Mathematics, 37
National Union of Students, 66
national standards, use of, 37
NCES. See National Center for Education Statistics
NCHEMS. See National Center for Higher Education Management
   Systems
Netherlands, 4
   performance indicators used to bring fiscal discipline, 5
   use of performance indicators, 68-72
networked organization, requirements of, 86

focus of, 49
four primary purposes of, 51
government involvement for, 49
in allocation of resources, 23
in dialogue, 23
in evaluation, 23
in rationalization, 23
intended audiences for, 50-51
intended elimination of quantitative measures, 77
locus of control of, 48-49
markets as locus of control for, 49
primary focus on monitoring existing systems, 79
problems in using, 89-92
relationship to institutional mission of, 51-52
sophisticated information technology association, 7
sources of variation in quality for, 49-50
such as teaching, research, and service, 64
suggestions in use of, 80-81
SUNY examples of, 17
system, 39
types in Australia, 64
types of, ix-x
United Kingdom use of, 56
use of term, 5
use of, 21-26, 48-52
Peterson's Guides in Princeton, 28, 91
planning and budgeting, link between not usually effective, 33
planning indicators of provinces in Canada, 61
Prairie View A&M University Research Enhancement Program, xiii
process measurement, efforts to address, 67
productive institution, definitions of, 13-14
productivity
        goals, 2
        problem with Finnish data on university, 73
Progressive Era, performance budgeting origin in, 33

Q

Quality Audit group, 58
quality assurance mechanism developed in Australia, 65
quality, study of what means in search for education indicators, 31
quantitative bias in data selection for performance indicators, 50
quantitative measures, three categories of, 55
Queen's University, ranking and comparisons with similar
    universities, 62

R

Reagan, Ronald, 6
Reauthorized Higher Education Act of 1965, 11

"report card bill," 7

S

Saint Louis University, x
SAT scores, ix
scholarships to white students to attend historically black
    college, 41
senior faculty teaching of lower division courses, 7
South Carolina
        collects information on involvement in sponsored
            research, 43
        institutional cost of measurement of performance, 12
        report cards on effectiveness used by, 2, 7
        senior faculty teaching lower division courses, 7
        state included in ECS project, 31
Southern Association of Colleges and Schools accreditation
    agency, 38
Southern Regional Education Board, 1
        model legislation preparation help by, 2
Special Development Plan for Higher Education, 73
special-purpose budget, 39-40
SREB. See Southern Regional Education Board
State University of New York, 6
        development of system wide set of performance
            indicators, 16-17, 21
        Distinguished Teaching Professorships, 15
        faculty role shift in, 13
        mission-driven indicators of, 90
Statistics Canada, 61
strategic indicators survey questionnaire, major headings
    of, 29-30
Student Financial Aid Program of Title IV, 11
Student Right-to-Know and Campus Security Act, 87
student funding as part of special purpose budget, 41
student total performance, reward or punish institutions for, 8
SUNY. See State University of New York
Sweden, use of performance indicators, 75-77

T

Tennessee
        goal-oriented performance funding model, 2
        Performance Funding Program, 25
        performance funding of, 33, 41
        senior faculty teaching lower division courses, 7
        state included in ECS project, 31
Texas
        A&M University, x
        faculty teaching time as performance indicator, 14

greater link between planning and budget allocations, 32-33

incentive funding consideration by, 2

performance indicator system for possible use in, 39, 40

possible performance funding experiment of, 33

scholarships to white students to attend historically black college, 41

senior faculty teaching lower division courses, 7

state included in ECS project, 31

Thatcher, Margaret, 6

U

U.S. Department of Education, 87

U.S. Higher Education Act, amendments encourage setting of standards, 87

undergraduate education,

development of "good practice indicators" for, 28

dominant focus will return to, 84

financial incentives against, 15

United Kingdom, 4

use of performance indicators, 6, 52-59

University Administration Act of 1970, 77

University of Miami, 89

University of Wisconsin

developing better measures of accountability, 34-36

rewarded with greater autonomy, 6

senior faculty teaching lower division courses, 7

V

Virginia

collects information on undergraduate integrative experiences, 43

competitive grants of, 40

higher education developing system of performance indicators, 34

report cards on effectiveness use of by, 2

small classes indicators, 43

state included in ECS project, 31

W

Webster University in Saint Louis, x

Winoma State University, 89

Wisconsin

small classes indicators, 43

state included in ECS project, 31

Working Party on Performance Indicators, 64, 65, 67

Y

yield ratio, 65

ASHE-ERIC HIGHER EDUCATION REPORTS

Since 1983, the Association for the Study of Higher Education (ASHE) and the Educational Resources Information Center (ERIC) Clearinghouse on Higher Education, a sponsored project of the Graduate School of Education and Human Development at The George Washington University, have cosponsored the *ASHE-ERIC Higher Education Report* series. The 1994 series is the twenty-third overall and the sixth to be published by the School of Education and Human Development at the George Washington University.

Each monograph is the definitive analysis of a tough higher education problem, based on thorough research of pertinent literature and institutional experiences. Topics are identified by a national survey. Noted practitioners and scholars are then commissioned to write the reports, with experts providing critical reviews of each manuscript before publication.

Eight monographs (10 before 1985) in the ASHE-ERIC Higher Education Report series are published each year and are available on individual and subscription bases. To order, use the order form on the last page of this book.

Qualified persons interested in writing a monograph for the ASHE-ERIC Higher Education Reports are invited to submit a proposal to the National Advisory Board. As the preeminent literature review and issue analysis series in higher education, we can guarantee wide dissemination and national exposure for accepted candidates. Execution of a monograph requires at least a minimal familiarity with the ERIC database, including *Resources in Education* and *Current Index to Journals in Education*. The objective of these Reports is to bridge conventional wisdom with practical research. Prospective authors are strongly encouraged to call Dr. Fife at 800-773-3742.

For further information, write to
ASHE-ERIC Higher Education Reports
The George Washington University
1 Dupont Circle, Suite 630
Washington, DC 20036
Or phone (202) 296-2597, toll-free: 800-773-ERIC.
Write or call for a complete catalog.

ADVISORY BOARD

Barbara E. Brittingham
University of Rhode Island

Mildred Garcia
Montclair State College

Rodolfo Z. Garcia
North Central Association of Colleges and Schools

James Hearn
University of Georgia

Bruce Anthony Jones
University of Pittsburgh

L. Jackson Newell
Deep Springs College

Carolyn Thompson
State University of New York–Buffalo

James Rhem
The National Teaching & Learning Forum

Gary Rhoades
University of Arizona

Scott Rickard
Association of College Unions–International

G. Jeremiah Ryan
Harford Community College

Patricia A. Spencer
Riverside Community College

Frances Stage
Indiana University–Bloomington

Kala M. Stroup
Southeast Missouri State University

Barbara E. Taylor
Association of Governing Boards

Carolyn J. Thompson
State University of New York–Buffalo

Sheila L. Weiner
Board of Overseers of Harvard College

Wesley K. Willmer
Biola University

Manta Yorke
Liverpool John Moores University

REVIEW PANEL

Charles Adams
University of Massachusetts–Amherst

Louis Albert
American Association for Higher Education

Richard Alfred
University of Michigan

Henry Lee Allen
University of Rochester

Philip G. Altbach
Boston College

Marilyn J. Amey
University of Kansas

Kristine L. Anderson
Florida Atlantic University

Karen D. Arnold
Boston College

Robert J. Barak
Iowa State Board of Regents

Alan Bayer
Virginia Polytechnic Institute and State University

John P. Bean
Indiana University–Bloomington

John M. Braxton
Peabody College, Vanderbilt University

Ellen M. Brier
Tennessee State University

Barbara E. Brittingham
The University of Rhode Island

Dennis Brown
University of Kansas

Peter McE. Buchanan
Council for Advancement and
    Support of Education

Patricia Carter
University of Michigan

John A. Centra
Syracuse University

Arthur W. Chickering
George Mason University

Darrel A. Clowes
Virginia Polytechnic Institute and State University

Deborah M. DiCroce
Piedmont Virginia Community College

Cynthia S. Dickens
Mississippi State University

Sarah M. Dinham
University of Arizona

Kenneth A. Feldman
State University of New York–Stony Brook

Dorothy E. Finnegan
The College of William & Mary

Mildred Garcia
Montclair State College

Rodolfo Z. Garcia
Commission on Institutions of Higher Education

Kenneth C. Green
University of Southern California

James Hearn
University of Georgia

Edward R. Hines
Illinois State University

Deborah Hunter
University of Vermont

Philo Hutcheson
Georgia State University

Bruce Anthony Jones
University of Pittsburgh

Elizabeth A. Jones
The Pennsylvania State University

Kathryn Kretschmer
University of Kansas

Marsha V. Krotseng
State College and University Systems of West Virginia

George D. Kuh
Indiana University–Bloomington

Daniel T. Layzell
University of Wisconsin System

Patrick G. Love
Kent State University

Cheryl D. Lovell
State Higher Education Executive Officers

Meredith Jane Ludwig
American Association of State Colleges and Universities

Dewayne Matthews
Western Interstate Commission for Higher Education

Mantha V. Mehallis
Florida Atlantic University

Toby Milton
Essex Community College

James R. Mingle
State Higher Education Executive Officers

John A. Muffo
Virginia Polytechnic Institute and State University

L. Jackson Newell
Deep Springs College

James C. Palmer
Illinois State University

Robert A. Rhoads
The Pennsylvania State University

G. Jeremiah Ryan
Harford Community College

Mary Ann Danowitz Sagaria
The Ohio State University

Daryl G. Smith
The Claremont Graduate School

William G. Tierney
University of Southern California

Susan B. Twombly
University of Kansas

Robert A. Walhaus
University of Illinois–Chicago

Harold Wechsler
University of Rochester

Elizabeth J. Whitt
University of Illinois–Chicago

Michael J. Worth
The George Washington University

RECENT TITLES

1994 ASHE-ERIC Higher Education Reports

1. The Advisory Committee Advantage: Creating an Effective Strategy for Programmatic Improvement
   by Lee Teitel

2. Collaborative Peer Review: The Role of Faculty in Improving College Teaching
   by Larry Keig and Michael D. Waggoner

3. Prices, Productivity, and Investment: Assessing Financial Strategies in Higher Education
   by Edward P. St. John

4. The Development Officer in Higher Education: Toward an Understanding of the Role
   by Michael J. Worth and James W. Asp, II

1993 ASHE-ERIC Higher Education Reports

1. The Department Chair: New Roles, Responsibilities and Challenges
   Alan T. Seagren, John W. Creswell, and Daniel W. Wheeler

2. Sexual Harassment in Higher Education: From Conflict to Community
   Robert O. Riggs, Patricia H. Murrell, and JoAnn C. Cutting

3. Chicanos in Higher Education: Issues and Dilemmas for the 21st Century
   by Adalberto Aguirre, Jr., and Ruben O. Martinez

4. Academic Freedom in American Higher Education: Rights, Responsibilities, and Limitations
   by Robert K. Poch

5. Making Sense of the Dollars: The Costs and Uses of Faculty Compensation
   by Kathryn M. Moore and Marilyn J. Amey

6. Enhancing Promotion, Tenure and Beyond: Faculty Socialization as a Cultural Process
   by William G. Tierney and Robert A. Rhoads

7. New Perspectives for Student Affairs Professionals: Evolving Realities, Responsibilities and Roles
   by Peter H. Garland and Thomas W. Grace

8. Turning Teaching Into Learning: The Role of Student Responsibility in the Collegiate Experience
   by Todd M. Davis and Patricia Hillman Murrell

1992 ASHE-ERIC Higher Education Reports

1. The Leadership Compass: Values and Ethics in Higher Education
   John R. Wilcox and Susan L. Ebbs

2. Preparing for a Global Community: Achieving an International Perspective in Higher Education
   Sarah M. Pickert

3. Quality: Transforming Postsecondary Education
   Ellen Earle Chaffee and Lawrence A. Sherr

4. Faculty Job Satisfaction: Women and Minorities in Peril
   Martha Wingard Tack and Carol Logan Patitu

5. Reconciling Rights and Responsibilities of Colleges and Students: Offensive Speech, Assembly, Drug Testing, and Safety
   Annette Gibbs

6. Creating Distinctiveness: Lessons from Uncommon Colleges and Universities
   Barbara K. Townsend, L. Jackson Newell, and Michael D. Wiese

7. Instituting Enduring Innovations: Achieving Continuity of Change in Higher Education
   Barbara K. Curry

8. Crossing Pedagogical Oceans: International Teaching Assistants in U.S. Undergraduate Education
   Rosslyn M. Smith, Patricia Byrd, Gayle L. Nelson, Ralph Pat Barrett, and Janet C. Constantinides

1991 ASHE-ERIC Higher Education Reports

1. Active Learning: Creating Excitement in the Classroom
   Charles C. Bonwell and James A. Eison

2. Realizing Gender Equality in Higher Education: The Need to Integrate Work/Family Issues
   Nancy Hensel

3. Academic Advising for Student Success: A System of Shared Responsibility
   Susan H. Frost

4. Cooperative Learning: Increasing College Faculty Instructional Productivity
   David W. Johnson, Roger T. Johnson, and Karl A. Smith

5. High School–College Partnerships: Conceptual Models, Programs, and Issues
   Arthur Richard Greenberg

6. Meeting the Mandate: Renewing the College and Departmental Curriculum
   William Toombs and William Tierney

7. Faculty Collaboration: Enhancing the Quality of Scholarship and Teaching
   Ann E. Austin and Roger G. Baldwin

8. Strategies and Consequences: Managing the Costs in Higher Education
   John S. Waggaman

1990 ASHE-ERIC Higher Education Reports

1. The Campus Green: Fund Raising in Higher Education
   Barbara E. Brittingham and Thomas R. Pezzullo

2. The Emeritus Professor: Old Rank - New Meaning
   James E. Mauch, Jack W. Birch, and Jack Matthews

3. "High Risk" Students in Higher Education: Future Trends
   Dionne J. Jones and Betty Collier Watson

4. Budgeting for Higher Education at the State Level: Enigma, Paradox, and Ritual
   Daniel T. Layzell and Jan W. Lyddon

5. Proprietary Schools: Programs, Policies, and Prospects
   John B. Lee and Jamie P. Merisotis

6. College Choice: Understanding Student Enrollment Behavior
   Michael B. Paulsen

7. Pursuing Diversity: Recruiting College Minority Students
   Barbara Astone and Elsa Nuñez-Wormack

8. Social Consciousness and Career Awareness: Emerging Link in Higher Education
   John S. Swift, Jr.

1989 ASHE-ERIC Higher Education Reports

1. Making Sense of Administrative Leadership: The 'L' Word in Higher Education
   Estela M. Bensimon, Anna Neumann, and Robert Birnbaum

2. Affirmative Rhetoric, Negative Action: African-American and Hispanic Faculty at Predominantly White Universities
   Valora Washington and William Harvey

3. Postsecondary Developmental Programs: A Traditional Agenda with New Imperatives
   Louise M. Tomlinson

4. The Old College Try: Balancing Athletics and Academics in Higher Education
   John R. Thelin and Lawrence L. Wiseman

5. The Challenge of Diversity: Involvement or Alienation in the Academy?
   Daryl G. Smith

6. Student Goals for College and Courses: A Missing Link in Assessing and Improving Academic Achievement
   Joan S. Stark, Kathleen M. Shaw, and Malcolm A. Lowther

7. The Student as Commuter: Developing a Comprehensive Institutional Response
   Barbara Jacoby

8. Renewing Civic Capacity: Preparing College Students for Service and Citizenship
   Suzanne W. Morse

1988 ASHE-ERIC Higher Education Reports

1. The Invisible Tapestry: Culture in American Colleges and Universities
   George D. Kuh and Elizabeth J. Whitt

2. Critical Thinking: Theory, Research, Practice, and Possibilities
   Joanne Gainen Kurfiss

3. Developing Academic Programs: The Climate for Innovation
   Daniel T. Seymour

4. Peer Teaching: To Teach is To Learn Twice
   Neal A. Whitman

5. Higher Education and State Governments: Renewed Partnership, Cooperation, or Competition?
   Edward R. Hines

6. Entrepreneurship and Higher Education: Lessons for Colleges, Universities, and Industry
   James S. Fairweather

7. Planning for Microcomputers in Higher Education: Strategies for the Next Generation
   Reynolds Ferrante, John Hayman, Mary Susan Carlson, and Harry Phillips

8. The Challenge for Research in Higher Education: Harmonizing Excellence and Utility
   Alan W. Lindsay and Ruth T. Neumann

*Out-of-print. Available through EDRS. Call 1-800-443-ERIC.

Quantity **Amount**

_____ Please begin my subscription to the 1994 *ASHE-ERIC Higher Education Reports* at $98.00, 31% off the cover price, starting with Report 1, 1994. Includes shipping. _____

_____ Please send a complete set of the 1993 *ASHE-ERIC Higher Education Reports* at $98.00, 31% off the cover price. Please add shipping charge, below. _____

Individual reports are avilable at the following prices:
1993 and 1994, $18.00; 1988–1992, $17.00; 1980–1987, $15.00

SHIPPING CHARGES
For orders of more than 50 books, please call for shipping information.

	1st three books	*Ea. addl. book*
U.S., 48 Contiguous States		
Ground:	$3.75	$0.15
2nd Day*:	8.25	1.10
Next Day*:	18.00	1.60
Alaska & Hawaii (2nd Day Only)*:	13.25	1.40

U.S. Territories and Foreign Countries: Please call for shipping information.
*Order will be shipping within 24 hours of request.
All prices shown on this form are subject to change.

PLEASE SEND ME THE FOLLOWING REPORTS:

Quantity	Report No.	Year	Title	Amount

Please check one of the following:
□ Check enclosed, payable to GWU–ERIC.
□ Purchase order attached ($45.00 minimum).
□ Charge my credit card indicated below:
   □ Visa   □ MasterCard

Subtotal: _____
Shipping: _____
Total Due: _____

Expiration Date _____

Name _____
Title _____
Institution _____
Address _____
City _____ State _____ Zip _____
Phone _____ Fax _____ Telex _____
Signature _____ Date _____

SEND ALL ORDERS TO: ASHE-ERIC Higher Education Reports
The George Washington University
One Dupont Cir., Ste. 630, Washington, DC 20036-1183
Phone: (202) 296-2597 • Toll-free: 800-773-ERIC